The Rubáiyát of Rumi

The Ergin Translations
Volume 1 of 4

The Rubáiyát of Rumi

The Ergin Translations
Volume 1 of 4

The Quatrains
from the
Osman-al Mavlavi Compilation
of
The Dîvân-i Kebîr of Mevlânâ Celâleddîn Rumi

Quatrains Compiled and Edited by
Millicent Alexander with Shahzad Mazhar

Introduction and Appendices by
Millicent Alexander

Powerhouse Publishing
Los Angeles, California
USA
www.ReadingRumi.com

Copyright © 2024 by Millicent Alexander

First published by Powerhouse Publishing 2024

All rights reserved. No part of this book may be reproduced or utilized in any form or by any means, electronic or mechanical, including photocopying, recording, or by any information storage and retrieval system, without permission in writing from the publisher.

Thank you for respecting the author's rights.

Printed in the United States of America.
ISBN: 978-1-947666-06-1 (hardcover)
ISBN: 978-1-947666-07-8 (paperback)
ISBN: 978-1-947666-08-5 (e-book)
Library of Congress Control Number: 2022938928

Available from Amazon.com and other retail outlets.
Printed, bound and distributed worldwide by IngramSpark.

Book design and layout by Oscar Díaz Del Valle and Toni Norcross.

Typeset in Schoolbook,
with Study and Duc de Berry as display type.

The cover artwork and the artwork on pages 1, 11, & 247 are photographs of the original artwork created by Abu Bekir al Mavlavi for the Osman-Al Mavlavi Compilation of the *Divân-i Kebîr* compiled in 1367-1368 CE and registered as #68 and #69 in the Mevlânâ Museum in Konya, Turkey. These photographs, as well as microfiche of the entire al Mavlavi compilation, were commissioned by Nevit O. Ergin with permission from the Turkish Ministry of Culture and the Mevlânâ Museum in Konya, Turkey.

Calligraphy and illustrations of the musical instruments, Kaaba and Whirling Dervish are by Smaro Gregoriadou.

In Memory
of
Hasan Lutfi Shushud

Gratitude

Ergin was deeply immersed in the essence of Rumi's works. We are eternally grateful for his making such a remarkable contribution to the English-speaking world. We are also eternally grateful for the opportunity he gave us to immerse ourselves for the past seven years in these quatrains.

We wish to express our gratitude, too, to Kavi Alexander, Yamil Alis, Zaid Alowayed, Kavous Barghi, Merâl Ekmekçioğlu, Banu, Evren and Zanep Ergin, Emre and Cengiz Ergin, Professor Mahmoud Ganadan, Jill Gluck, Edmond Gorginian, Jeferson Martinez, Toni Norcross, Haydar Pekdemir, Amy and Amit Singh, and especially: Oscar Díaz del Valle, John Morris, Dimitris Economidis and Smaro Gregoriadou.

Contents

Introduction 1
    Foreword 3
    Mevlânâ Celâleddîn Rumi 7

The Rubáiyát 11

Appendices 247
    Notes on these Translations 249
    The Importance of Islam in Rumi's Life 259
    Islamic and Sufi Terms Commonly Used in Rumi's Poetry 261
    The Role of Music in Rumi's Life 263
    Musical Instruments Commonly Referred to in Rumi's Poetry. 265
    The Story of Joseph and Jacob 268
    The Concordance 270
    Bibliography: *Mevlânâ Rubâîler* 286
    Bibliography: *The Rubáiyát of Rumi, The Ergin Translations* .. 287

There is a sea which is not far from us.

It is unseen, but it is not hidden.

It is forbidden to talk about,

yet, at the same time,

it is a sin and a sign of ungratefulness not to.

-*Dîvân-i Kebîr,* Volume 1
ghazal 97, verse 1205

Introduction

Rumi climbed the mountain. Rumi was the mountain. May Rumi be known.

-Nevit Ergin

Foreword

Since Rumi's passing in 1273, every century has been a good one for exploring his wisdom, because truth does not age. Even so, considering all of the divisions and challenges we are currently facing, there has never been a better time than today to get to know him...or to get to know him better.

There are those who are satisfied with this world and the notion that we are here to attain worldly happiness. Rumi is considered to be a brilliant poet, and so reading Rumi's rubáiyát [collection of quatrains] is for them.

There are those who are born with an uneasiness, a restless soul which searches for the beyond. For their understanding of the universe and eternity, they often turn to philosophy, psychology, science, religion and other disciplines which depend on gathering information, reaching out and pulling in. Rumi's rubáiyát is for them. His rubáiyát is filled with all kinds of wisdom and information, giving us a rich historical context and psychological insights into life in 13th century Asia Minor. Much of what he shares is as relevant today as it was then.

Yet, as Rumi tells us, most of the explorations taken up in this world are dead-end streets:

> O heart, you go nowhere on this road
> with talk and gossip.
> You cannot reach the Beloved
> unless you pass through the door of Absence.
> O heart, you must take to the air
> where His birds fly.
> Otherwise, they will not grant you wings.
>
> -Rubai 247 (Volume 1)

He tells us that the beyond is inside of us, but to reach it, we must embark on a long, challenging journey:

> The secret of Truth cannot be understood
> by asking questions, gathering information,
> or spending all your wealth and belongings.
> If you haven't cried for fifty years
> with bloody tears,
> if you haven't burned your heart out,
> you will not find the way
> from this world to ecstasy.
>
> -Rubai 609 (Volume 2)

For those uneasy souls who do embark on this journey, Rumi's rubáiyát is for them. His rubáiyát offers signposts of progress all along the way, from the beginning to the end and everywhere in between.

Some of the verses are wildly earthly, filled with advice on how one should act in this world. Some are instructions for making the journey. Some are motivational. Some are prayers. Some describe intense suffering. Some are filled with longing. Some express nothing less than the attainment of the divine. All of them reflect Rumi's courageous journey.

Although our external journey is unique to each of us, the need to take an internal journey is the same. And make no mistake: Rumi is very clear about the importance of embarking, no matter what one's age:

> Take up your arms.
> This is the time for war, O soul.
> It is getting late. Don't hesitate.
> This world is nothing but a colorful show.

> Give it up, O soul.
> There is a cat and mouse fight
> on every corner, O soul.
>> -Rubai 792 (Volume 2)

What steps are needed to start the journey? On the Itlak Sufi Path of Annihilation and Liberation which Ergin practiced, there are only four elements: fasting, a type of rhythmic breathing, suffering, and least important, discussion.

What does Rumi say about fasting?

> It is customary for Love
> to eat the essence of faith for Its meals.
> Love goes after neither bread
> nor the worries of life.
> Its table is set beyond day and night.
> Then, what is fasting?
> It is an invitation to Love's secret feast.
>> -Rubai 773 (Volume 2)

As for suffering:

> The nicest thing about Love
> is that it is the source of troubles.
> One is not a lover if he fears troubles.
> One has to be brave in the business of Love.
> When his soul catches the fire of Love,
> a lover has to give up his soul.
>> -Rubai 435 (Volume 1)

And although the traveler and the traveler alone can do the work of the journey, Rumi is clear that help comes from the beyond:

> If you start the journey,
> they will open the road for you.
> If you annihilate your self,
> they will carry you to Absence.
> Humble yourself, and they will grow you
> greater than the Universe.
> Become nothing,
> and they will show You without you.
>
> -Rubai 276 (Volume 1)

Rumi also clearly describes what happens to the persevering traveler on this journey to Absence:

> There is nothing remaining in my ears
> except Love's murmur.
> There is nothing remaining in my soul,
> no reason, no thought,
> only the sweetness of Eternity.
> The colorless brush of Love has mixed all colors.
> Now, not even the remembrance of color remains.
>
> -Rubai 1776 (Volume 4)

In total, there are 1,867 quatrains which we are publishing in four volumes. They are not in the order in which Rumi shared them with those around him, but rather in the order in which they were compiled by Osman-al Mavlavi in 1367-1368 CE. Whether each volume is read from beginning to end or whether verses are simply chosen at random, we hope these remarkable writings become your dear friends.

Mevlânâ Celâleddîn Rumi

Image Credit: The Granger Collection, Ltd.,
Historical Picture Archive/NY.

Mevlânâ Celâleddîn Rumi

His full name is Mevlânâ Celâleddîn Muhammed Rumi [Turkish], or Master Jalal of Rum. The Islamic world knows him as Mowlānā [Our Master]. The West knows him as Rumi. His poetry is beautiful and inspired, reaching the pinnacle of the rich Persian poetic tradition. But, to call him a great poet is an unfortunate understatement. Perhaps no other human has, through his own words, given us such a clear view into the journey of a mystic on the road to Absence, to the Divinity, to Nothingness.

Rumi was born in present-day Afghanistan in 1207 and lived most of his life in Konya, Turkey, where he died in 1273. He was a Muslim scholar, well-respected in his community by those from all walks of life, including imams, priests and rabbis, beggars and Seljuk royalty.

The life event which is most remarked upon by today's scholars, translators, and commentators is his meeting in 1244 with the Sufi mystic Shams of Tabriz (1185-1248). The two spent less than three years together, yet Shams was able to transform Rumi into an ecstatic lover of God. After meeting Shams, to quote Rumi:

> I burned down my store,
>
> my business and profession.
>
> I learned how to write verses, odes and quatrains.
>
> Love is in my soul, my heart and my eyes.
>
> And, since I have fallen in Love,
>
> I have burned out all three of these.

-Rubai 727 (Volume 2)

Now, almost 800 years later, thanks to his meeting Shams, mankind is still being blessed with the vastness of Rumi's wisdom.

For those who are unfamiliar with Rumi's history or the history of Shams of Tabriz, there are well-researched books and articles available. Our focus here is on his quatrains and the reflection of the journey which they create, because as Rumi states:

> Absence is the real treasure.
>
> To reach it is the purpose of this world.
>
> -Rubai 584 (Volume 2)

Learn from the One
who is the essence of the Book,
the meaning of this writing.

-Dîvân-i Kebîr, Volume 8
ghazal 20, verse 190

The Rubáiyát

O Beloved, when Your Love flared up in my heart,
everything else was burned to ashes.
My heart put my mind, books and lessons on a shelf
and replaced them all with poetry.

      -Rubai 362 (Volume 1)

Love's fire warms the whole world.   1
Love delivers suffering out of kindness.
The Moon of Love makes even the Sun feel ashamed.
How impudent is the man
who is not ashamed in front of that Moon!

My essence has been gripped and pulsed   2
by pure, clean, ruby-colored wine.
My glass yells and screams from the pressure.
But, I have been drinking that wine
glass after glass after glass
for so long
that that wine has come into me
and I have gone into that wine.

3   How regretful that so much time has passed.
    Yet, we are still crazy, insane with Love.
    It is a dark, foggy night and we cannot see the shore.
    But, we are sailing in a ship on God's boundless sea
    thanks to the grace, help and kindness of God.

4   Come. The glory of your true face cannot be hidden.
    Come. Your Beauty is not made by man's semen.
    Come. Don't hide yourself behind anger.
    Come. Your Beauty cannot be concealed.

The original words are given life by the eternal Soul,   5
that Soul which has no color,
yet which gives the gift of color
and which gives strength to the torch of faith.
We spoke much, but we did not speak about that.

"Beloved, what is the best job for a fig seller?"   6
"Naturally, O my soul, to sell figs."
"And for us, it is living drunk, dying drunk,
and running to resurrection as a drunk.
That is the job most suitable for us, O Beloved."

7   First, He pampered me with a thousand favors.
    Then, He burned me with a thousand troubles.
    He played with me
    as if I were nothing more than dice
    in His game of Love.
    But, when I died from myself and became Him,
    He finally threw me out.

8   This fire of Love cooks and matures us,
    pulling us every night to the tavern,
    separating us from others.
    Love makes us friends with only those of the tavern.

O the greenness of every tree,   9
the greenness of every garden and orchard,
every grass and meadow,
O my glory, fate and greatness,
O my solitude, my Sema, my honesty, my deceit,
without You, all these words are empty. Come!

O swaying cypress,   10
may autumn winds never harm You.
O eye of the Universe, may evil's eye never see You.
You are the soul of the Earth and the sky.
May nothing but compassion and sweetness
ever touch Your soul!

11   One who accepts our creed and walks our way
sees so many naked souls in our body.
One who drinks sherbet from our glass
becomes so drunk that he sees our night as day.

12   O Beloved, the night Moon rose,
but could find no trace of You.
Because You are such a Moon as that,
gifts are given
to those who circle around You at night.
Even the dawn, which colors everything red,
is check-mated by Your pale face.

My Beloved whose scattered hair   13
makes everyone confused,
whose sweet ruby lips drip honey,
that Beloved asked me,
"Are you sorry about our separation?"
I answered, "O my soul, so very much so
that all the world's sorrows are in that sorry."

O one who sacrifices the pearl of faith   14
for a loaf of bread,
O one who sacrifices the essence of his heart
for a piece of barley,
like you, Nimrod[1] kept his heart from Abraham,
and, in the end, gave it to a gnat instead.

---

[1] The tyrannical king responsible for building the Tower of Babel. Refers to the story of Abraham and the casting out of idols. Quran 21:58-69. Further, according to legend, Nimrod assembled an army to challenge Abraham, but Abraham produced an army of gnats. One entered Nimrod's ear and drove him out of his mind.

15   O fickle fortune of the heavens, you are disturbing
     the peace and comfort of my heart
     with all kinds of tricks and deceits.
     But, there will be a day when I sit at your table.
     On that day you will see
     how I can make polished bowls from moonlight.

16   I placed my heart on the way of troubles,
     untying its feet so it could run after You.
     The wind brought Your scent today.
     In gratitude, I gave my heart to the wind.

With Love, we are going on our mounts 17
to the land of Absence.
Our night is illuminated by the wine of Union,
that divine wine which is permitted in our faith.
Our lips won't become dry for even one moment
until we reach the morning of Absence.

I can't sleep on the nights I am with you 18
because of my joy and pleasure.
I can't sleep on the nights I am separated from you,
because of my weeping and wailing.
I am awake throughout both of these nights
thanks to the blessing of God.
But, the difference between them is amazing.

19 As long as the Beloved's image remains with us,
we are in good shape, O heart.
No matter where that image appears,
when the heart gets another thorn,
that thorn is better than a thousand sweet dates.

20 Since God made early separation our fate,
what was the use of all those fights and fears?
If I was bad,
then now you are saved from all that.
If I was good,
then remember our good conversations.

I don't have any friend besides Love.   21
Love was with me before I came into this world,
and Love is still with me.
My soul is yelling,
"O lazy one on Love's way, come on.
Hurry up. Reach me."

I should use all my cunning and, as a drunk,   22
throw myself into the sky
to see if that Beauty of the Universe is there.
If He is, I will attain my desire.
If not, I will lose my head like I lost my heart.

23   A certain One's cunning made me clap my hands,
        made me shameless, blind, unable to think.
        In short, His heart turned my heart inside out
        to make it into the way He wanted it to be.

24   Smoke from our heart
        is the sign of our Love, O heart!
        Smoke which comes from a heart is obvious, O heart!
        Such a heart is turning into a rough sea
        with waves of blood, O heart!

Never let grief enter into you, O heart!   25
Don't go to the assembly of the ones
with whom you are not intimate.
Since you are satisfied
with dry bread and a bunch of cress,
don't consider swaggering in the world
like the spike on the tip of an ear of corn.

On the night of Union,   26
the lover searches for that Beauty.
If some dust of His trace doesn't appear,
that lover loses his way.
All the stars appear to be upside down.
But, on such a night of Union
it is difficult to see another at such close range.

27   A lover should be crazy-insane,
     scorned, disgraced, and drunk all year long.
     We are susceptible to suffering when we are awake.
     But, when we are drunk, everything is good.

28   The path of our Prophet is Love.
     We are the children of Love.
     Our mother is Love,
     that mother who is hidden in the dress of our flesh,
     hiding from our deceitful, incapable self.

Love for You kills Turks as well as non-Turks.   29
We are slaves and servants
to those martyrs, those generals.
Love says,
"No one escapes Me. I own all souls."
He is right, O heart.
Quit playing.

We haven't seen Your rose garden for such a long time.   30
We haven't been able to catch
Your wine-making narcissus eyes.
You are concealed from creation, the same way loyalty is.
We haven't seen Your face for such a long, long time.

31   Once life ends,
God gives another life, a different one.
Once this temporary life is annihilated,
there is a permanent one.
Love is the Water of Life. Plunge into it.
There is a new life in every drop of that sea.

32   Sometimes, angels are jealous of our purity.
Sometimes, the devil is afraid of our recklessness.
Our clay body carries God's gift.
Bravos to our power and abilities.

When I die, 33
place my body next to my Beloved.
If He kisses my pale lips,
don't be surprised if I come back to life.

Time will cut short this uproar. 34
The wolf of death will tear this flock to pieces.
Everyone carries some pride,
some illusion of greatness in his head.
But, the slap of death always arrives sooner or later.

35 I was heart and soul without a body before,
    pure, clean, pleasant.
    My Master built my body as a guest house
    and put my soul in it.
    If You are so kind, do me a favor!
    Pardon me.
    Recreate me as You did before.
    Bring me back to life.

36 I have tested my beautiful, good-natured Beloved.
    No torrent of water has ever muddied His river.
    He hasn't frowned once,
    not even once throughout an entire day.
    I will love him always, alive or dead.

My Master, I repent for the past.   37
Will You pardon a lover who has been long gone?
If my repentance is an insolence,
may God forgive me,
God forgive me,
God forgive me!

O traveler, what is your intention?   38
Where are you going?
No matter where you go, your place is in our heart.
How long will you twitch with sorrow
like a fish out of water,
stranded on rough, wet stones?
Your lips are dry, yet you remain on the river bank.
How long do you intend to stay there?

39   La hawla[2] helps men deal with this life's troubles.
But, La hawla also increases sorrows.
Many sorrows, many troubles
come from the breath of La hawla.
So what exactly is La hawla?

40   At first, like others, I preferred being my self.
Although I was aware of my existence,
I did not comprehend my being.
Because I could not see, I did not recognize who I was.
I was merely hearing my name.
Finally, and only when I went out of my self completely,
I saw my real being.

---

[2][Arabic] "La hawla va la kuwwata illa billah." Praise and submission. "There is no strength or power but in God." Mentioned by a Muslim when facing a calamity or situation he cannot control. A variant can be found in Quran 18:39.

The Moses of this flock has a strange staff.   41
When He strikes it on the ground,
it wipes away all these fantasies.
It eliminates feasting and wars.
Few minds will understand this.

Like every other day, we are desperately in Love today.   42
Don't open the door of thoughts.
Play the rebab whose sound makes us forget everything.
There are a hundred different prayers and prostrations
for the one whose mihrab,[3] whose alter
is the Beauty of the Beloved.

---

[3][Arabic] A niche in the wall of a mosque or religious school indicating the direction of Mecca, which Muslims face when praying.

43   For the sake of the hearts of your friends,
don't sleep tonight.
Grab night's ear and twist it. Don't sleep!
Although it is said
that a trouble-maker is better when he is sleeping,
it would be better for a trouble-maker like you
to stay awake.
So, stay awake! Don't sleep!

44   Wherever wine, rebab and kebab exist,
anxiety and thoughts cannot enter or endure.
O friends, let yourself be submerged in immortal joy.
Kiss the banks of that river like grass and roses do.

O heart, for a few nights, don't sleep until dawn.   45
Be like the moon separated from the sun.
Don't sleep.
Like a bucket, walk in the darkness of the well,
so it may happen that you rise again.

The flowers of the pomegranate   46
have become slaves and servants of your face.
Don't sleep!
O delight of spring and the rose garden,
don't sleep!
O sleepy, blood-thirsty, narcissus eyes,
don't sleep!
Tonight is the night of joy and wine-drinking.
Don't sleep!

47 O moon-faced one, don't sleep tonight!
Start turning like the whirling sky. Don't sleep!
Our wakefulness is a lamp for the Universe.
For this one night, watch that lamp.
Don't sleep!

48 Beloved, there is no one like You. Please don't sleep!
You put everything in perfect order.
Tonight, hundreds of candles
will be lit from Your light.
Please, do us a favor: don't sleep!

You are such an existence   49
that even the sky rejoices because of You.
Is it a surprise
that a human has fallen in Love with You?
I will be Your slave, Your servant as long as I live.
Whenever and whatever You want,
I will always do what You require of me.

Tonight, lift up all curtains immediately.   50
Give up both worlds so that not even a hair remains.
Last night, You were talking
about the soul and the heart.
Tonight, I will put both of them in front of You.
One will be cut into pieces.
The other will be constantly crying.

51   Our wine is continually served without cup or glass.
Our heart burns in our chest without smoke.
Love and sorrow keep crying and wailing,
but their song doesn't come from the rebab.
It comes from His bow and plectrum instead.

52   At our gathering, we don't need wine to get drunk.
Nor do we need harp or rebab to find joy.
Without cupbearer, musician or beauties
we have fallen on the floor,
out of ourselves like drunks.

Sleep tried to enter through my eyes,   53
but it couldn't find a place to settle,
because, thanks to You,
they were filled with fire and water.
Then, sleep moved towards my heart.
But, my heart was being crazy-insane, like mercury.
So then, sleep turned to my body to settle there.
But, my body was in ruins, completely in ruins!

Do you understand what the sound of the rebab says?   54
It says, "Look inside of your heart
to find the right way."
You have made inadvertent blunders on this way.
Those blunders will lead you to rightness.
Questions on this way will lead you to perfect answers.

55 Praise God! You and I are bright pearls.
    We are also opposites of each other in every way.
    I am your fate and I do not dream.
    You are my fate
    and you stay inside of the world of dreams.

56 If you want true happiness and immortal life,
    don't sleep!
    Burn with the fire of the Beloved. Don't sleep!
    You have slept hundreds of nights,
    and what have you found?
    For God's sake, stay awake for one night until dawn.
    Don't sleep!

O sleep, even if you were to become   57
the sweet Water of Life,
we wouldn't want to deal with you tonight.
And tonight, even if you had as many heads
as you have hairs,
you could not scratch even one of them, O sleep.

The ones who know the secret   58
have become drunk tonight.
They are sitting behind the curtain
with the Beloved tonight.
O outsider, go away.
It is unpleasant to be with strangers tonight.

59 Yes, my beloved,
    since you don't have any other good excuse,
    you are now running away from me, saying,
    "I feel sleepy."
    Go. Sleep well.
    I will cry about those sleepy, narcissus eyes until dawn.

60 Since we see others, we are not one anymore.
    We are in the business of the many.
    We identify good and bad,
    and that is where the trouble begins.
    A heart which has not reached ecstasy
    will keep getting kicked by the other.

There is a plain beyond belief and disbelief. 61
Our Love stands in the middle of that plain.
The sage will prostrate there,
because there is no room for belief or disbelief there.

Your heart has raised 62
so many plots and deceptions
that you both have fallen from the favor of Grace.
As when the Pharaoh did not acknowledge
the one true God,
when your heart seized the world,
the world became seized by freezing snow.

63 I can easily give up all desires and wishes.
    But, it is impossible
    to separate from the One who is the Soul of our soul.
    Everyone leaves others in service to Him.
    But, who could ever leave Him?
    Who could separate from Him?

64 My eyes are shedding so many tears
    because of being separated from You.
    My heart is longing for You.
    Alas! Will our time which has already passed
    ever return?

Peaceful and happy is the one   65
who is not bound by wealth or poverty, by more or less,
who doesn't care about this world
or about the people of this world,
who is without, in fact,
even the smallest particle of his self.

After my heart threw me into chaos, it ran away.   66
After my soul saw the intensity of my Love, it ran away.
After hearing my cry, Venus appeared with her harp.
But, after seeing me on fire, she put down her harp.
Then she, too, ran away.

67   My moon-faced One has come, clapping His hands.
He has come like soul, open and obvious,
and at the same time, secret and hidden.
My Beloved has come as a drunk, happy and joyful.
I am like this, because He has come like that.

68   Tonight is the soul of all nights.
Tonight, all prayers are accepted.
Tonight is the night of the offering and receiving
of blessings.
Tonight is the night of the One
who is close to the secrets of God.

He approached me, 69
because he thought I had gold in my hand.
Since I had no gold, he left quickly.
Once he gave his ear to the world of gold,
that gold became an earring[4] of slavery for him.

Be fair. Love is a beautiful thing. 70
Troubles come from the bad intentions
of our human nature.
You gave the name of Love to your lust.
But, there is a long way from lust to Love.

---

[4]In the medieval Islamic world, the wearing of an earring indicated that the wearer was a slave.

71   He is inside and outside of my heart.
He is the soul of my body.
He is my blood and my veins.
How could faith or heresy fit here?
I am absent. He is all of my existence.

72   When God gives someone a Beloved like You,
He makes that one's heart and soul restless, unstable.
Don't expect normal behavior from him.
God has assigned him an unusual task
in the business of Love.

That Beloved 73
who was the Beauty of our gathering
has gone.
He is not around now, and I don't know where He is.
He was the tallest, most dignified cypress.
For us, His leaving was like Qayamat![5]

The guide whose soul walks in front 74
of the ranks of lovers
knows well that You are the ocean,
and the Universe is the foam of that ocean.
You have a lover who dances
without ney or tambourine.
What will he do tonight?
There are neys and tambourines everywhere tonight!

---

[5][Arabic] The Day of Resurrection when the Earth will be torn apart.

75 That Master was carrying a load of pure sugar,
but He was so intoxicated
that He was unaware of His load.
I asked Him, "Is that sugar in my fate, too?"
He answered, "No."
But, He was unaware that His "no"
was just like sugar to me!

76 Who is He who gives pleasure to the body?
Who is He that color and shape
become blurry without Him?
One moment, He hides in shape and body.
The next, He rises from the Land of Absence
and reflects on those very same forms.

When the soul which has been bound 77
by the colors and shapes of material attributes
is ascending to Essence
by the light of the Prophet Muhammad,
while rising, it is pronouncing "Peace be upon Him"[6]
to bless Muhammad's soul.

Who is He who brings us the pleasure of Sema? 78
Who is He who takes the joy of the gathering with Him
when He leaves?
In order to prove that ney and tambourine
are not the source of happiness,
sometimes He comes and goes from Sema secretly.

---

[6]An Arabic phrase of veneration, or durood, attached to the names of holy figures in Islam.

79 That Sultan doesn't turn His face away
    from bad-mannered creatures.
    He tolerates
    hundreds of shameless people like you.
    Let His ocean-like Grace hear these words:
    "Although even Satan runs away from our darkness,
    He never does."

80 He is with us, that secret, beautiful face
    which refreshes joy and pleasure,
    which illuminates the Universe.
    We should hold onto Him tightly today.
    Yesterday is gone and so is the day before.
    Today is now the only day.

He is such a Sultan that wherever He stands,   81
that ground turns into a crown.
I said to Him, "Our separation is worse than my death.
Here is my pale face as proof."
He answered, "Go away. Your face has become pale
because of Love.
You have no reason to complain."

The one who sees You with the eyes of his head   82
is actually laughing at his own beard and mustache.
That poor one who compares himself with You
has such thorns in his eyes!

83   This is not spring. It is a different season.
The spark in every eye comes from a different union.
All the branches are moving,
but each one moves
thanks to a different wind, a different reason.

84   There is a close Friend inside of you
who gives you breath, life
and even the hope of reaching the Sacred Place.
Drink the wine He offers you until your last breath,
because this comes from His Grace and generosity,
not from any whims or playful behaviors.

Whose wine cannot be poured into glasses? 85
Whose worldly trap has caught us like birds?
Whose sugars, almonds and pistachios are those,
scattered for lovers every moment, everywhere?

What is this mischief in my wearied heart? 86
Why does Love bend my back like a harp?
Why does my true heart which is inside of me
fight with me for Him day and night?

87 Today, my heart is full of my Beloved's teaching.
My fever has not come from daily work,
but from His heat.
The doctor said, "Do such and such."
I am abstaining from everything the doctor prescribed,
except the wine and sugar from my Beloved's lips.

88 Not everyone looks for You.
Not every mill wheel turns by the water
coming from Your river.
Not everyone can draw a strong, tight bow.
For that, one has to be a Rostam.[7]

---

[7] A Persian king who became a legendary and mythical hero with great powers.

This Love is such a Sultan, but His banner is invisible. 89
This is such a Quran, but its verses are invisible.
This Hunter wounds every lover,
but the blood from those wounds is invisible.

O one who has been deceived by flesh, 90
who doesn't know His own essence,
put your mind in your head.
The Beloved is inside of you.
Senses are the essence of the body.
The essence of your senses is your soul.
If you go beyond body, senses and soul,
everything is the Beloved.

91   O Beauty, no one in this world is as pure and clean
      as You are.
      No one is more beautiful, elegant or charming
      than You.
      On the way of Love,
      there will always be accusations and recriminations.
      But, as long as You are my friend,
      that is enough for me.

92   O ruby, O agate, O pearl. O sea of meaning, O pure gold!
      You have no place, yet You stand firmly in Truth
      and never turn from God's way.
      O master of the soul who adds Soul to soul,
      if lateness suits You,
      come late, as long as You come safely.

O Joseph, your father's home is the safest place for you.   93
The plains and your brothers' homes are full of danger.
It is safer to befriend a wolf
than to spend your time with those envious ones!
An envious wolf is far worse
than a savage wolf of the plains.

O body, as long as you have such a soul, you will not die!   94
O unbeliever, rejoice. Faith is with you!
Although you have become tired and weak from lust,
by nature, you are a true man,
so, the fortitude of the brave ones is with you!

95   O heart, here you are,
sitting in the middle of His sorrow, His troubles.
To suffer is the cure. Do not complain.
That is the order.
When you step on the head of your desire,
your dog-self will be suffocated.
That is the sacrifice.

96   O mortal, this is the Master of all the East.
This is the lightning
from the cloud which scatters pearls.
Whatever you say is based on reasoning alone,
whereas He tells what He sees,
and that is the difference.

O beautiful One, every Beauty in this world   97
is longing for You.
O beautiful One, Your eyebrow
is the direction of prayer for the devout.
I have undressed from all of my attributes
in order to swim naked in Your beautiful river.

O body, O donkey,   98
are you aware of the One whom you carry?
There is a peerless Beauty on your back.
Rather than the Earth, step on the Throne.
Even the Sun cannot look upon the face
of that One you carry on your back.

99 If I turn around You
    there is cupbearer, glass and wine.
    When You manifest,
    my soul is bewildered and lost in amazement
    as it was for Moses, son of Imran.

100 There is no better friendship than having no friend.
    There is no better job than having no job.
    To give up tricks and deceits,
    by God, that is by far the best trick,
    the cleverest trick of them all.

O soul, O Universe,   101
souls and the Universe are temporary.
There is no Beauty, no cupbearer except Eternal Love.
A lover turns around the sacred house of Absence.
He is from that sacred house, not from the surroundings,
so for him, there is no horizon.

O one who looks for straw and barley like a donkey!   102
How long will time's groom be training you?
Since every foul mouth tastes your lips,
how could you ever expect
to receive a kiss from that Beauty?

103 The Water of Life is a drop of water
from Your beautiful face.
The Moon in the sky is the pale reflection
of Your bright countenance.
I said, "I want moonlight all night long
on this long night."
The night is the darkness of Your hair.
The moonlight is the brilliance of Your face.

104 O one whose thoughts are bound, your feet are free.
And, there is a secret in movement, in action.
With movement, boredom turns into joy.
That is why the water of a fountain or river
is better than the water of a stagnant pond.

His feet used to walk drunkenly   105
through the rose garden
while his hands were gathering roses.
When the trap of death was opened and closed,
those hands were cut, those feet broken.

If a person doesn't ease your heart,   106
doesn't please your soul,
if he doesn't let you free yourself
from the mud of humanity,
stay away from him.
Otherwise, the souls of saints will not forgive you.

107   If a friend has become intimate with my enemy,
it is no longer appropriate to sit next to him.
Stay away from the rose which is close to the thorn.
Avoid the fly which is friendly with a snake.

108   Your soul is a guest of your body
for only a couple of days.
Yet, you have become so attached to this Earth
that you don't want to listen when I talk about death.
Your soul is longing for that mansion,
that "death before death."[8]
Unfortunately, your body's donkey
has fallen asleep in the middle of the road.

---

[8] Annihilation of the self before the death of the body.

I asked the ney, "Why are you complaining?   109
How can you wail and cry
when you have lost nothing?"
The ney answered, "They cut and separated me
from a sugar-lipped one.
That is why I cannot live without wail and cry."

A Cavalier of Absence   110
has raised dust and galloped away.
He has gone, but the dust remains.
O one who is searching for God and Truth,
don't look to the right or to the left.
Stay on the road.
His dust is here,
but He is in the Land of Absence.

111   The one who enters the Sultan's tent
       does so only
       with the permission and blessing of the Sultan.
       The door of the Sultan cannot be reached
       merely by being out of one's self.
       There are thousands of paths leading
       to that out-of-self state.

112   Much gusto is on display at the table of Eternity.
       Those at the table eat.
       They are still eating and always will.
       But, the table remains the same.
       Nothing is ever diminished.
       When a bird lands on the top of a mountain,
       then flies away,
       the mountain remains that same mountain.

My Beloved has closed the door of union to me.   113
He has broken my heart with bitter words
and much sorrow.
Since my Beloved likes to see broken hearts,
since He keeps them as friends,
I will sit at His door broken-hearted.

Mistakes and sins are written in our fate.   114
Because of Love, we are drunk, exuberant
and have a bad reputation.
But, O Beloved, since You are the source
of our existence and our longing,
we have no reason to complain.
You are the source of it all.

115   Get up. Keep going around this Kaaba.

Keep turning around Him, like a pilgrim at Arafat.[9]

Why are you stuck on this ground like mud?

Don't you know that movement

is a key to abundance?

116   Wherever I put my head down on the ground,

He is the One who is prostrated.

He is the one worshiped

in these six dimensions[10] and beyond.

All I speak about,

the rose gardens, the nightingales, the beauties,

all are just pretext.

The only object, the only purpose is Him.

---

[9] A plain near Mecca where pilgrims gather as a stop on their way to the Kaaba.
[10] The material realm.

The uproar which is rising to the sky 117
is caused by the Love for His face.
The heart hears praises
which proclaim the beauty of His cheeks.
The soul is filled with jugs of His wine.
The heart's neck is chained by the curls of His hair.

There is a Beauty in my heart who is envied 118
by even the fairest of beauties.
As long as this is so, who could be happier than I am?
I have heard of something called sorrow.
Thank God, I don't know what that is.

119   It seems like this Earth is unconscious.
But, like a rabbit, its eyes are merely closed
as if it is sleeping.
It is like a saucepan with bubbles rising to the top,
so that creation may know it is boiling.

120   As long as the sun of the soul shines,
Sufis will dance around it like particles.
Some say, "That is the devil's business."
What a beautiful devil it must be
which gives Soul to souls!

This whirling, mirror-like sky raises waves of blood   121
in the heart of Love.
Some days they are visible, some days not.
But, they are there working day and night.

Don't sit idle as long as   122
even a trace of existence remains in you.
You are still worshiping idols.
Even if you do break doubt and suspicion
with the axe of reason,
you are simply creating a new idol
called self-confidence.

123   When frightened, a real lover who rides towards God
      cannot be separated from the Beloved
      by the threats of enemies.
      A real lover will not give up Truth
      for something which comes straight
      from the imagination.

124   Why should I repent?
      My repentance comes from You.
      In fact, the whole of repentance comes from You.
      It is the biggest sin to repent in front of You.
      Is there any repentance
      which deserves to appear in front of You?

The heart of remorse is like iron.   125
It opens its eyes with anger and wants to kill me.
I am lost in the curls of Your hair.
But, what remorse wants to do to me, I will do to him.

"As long as I live, I won't stray from the right way."   126
That's the oath I gave to myself.
I looked to my right, then to my left,
then to my right, then to my left,
then to my right, then to my left,
until finally,
I saw nothing except my Beloved.

127   The world isn't worth half a grain of barley.
      You are the gold mine.
      You are the Essence and the purpose
      of the Universe.
      Everything is created for You.
      If the world were illuminated by torches and candles,
      what would be their use without a lighter?
      The wind would put all of them out.

128   Our soul has turned into a stranger.
      Our sensible mind has become useless, crazy-insane.
      The Sultan's treasure is buried in ruins.
      Our heart has become the ruins of ruins
      all for the sake of that treasure.

When a soul drinks Love's wine   129
from the vineyard of that Beauty,
that vineyard grabs him by the throat and says,
"You drank my blood. Now, I will drink yours."

Whatever my complaints are, O Beloved,   130
Your sorrow is worse than that.
Your sorrow is like heartache, fever,
the pain of the body, bitter grief.
Everything is consumed and decreased
except for your sorrow.
That is only increasing.

131 My soul turned to the Beloved's soul,
making that its direction of prayer,
prostrating before Him.
All this came to us thanks to the Sultan
who sits on the soul's throne.
He is the One who runs the whole show.

132 There is a Beauty who had been playing nightly
a beautiful, harmonious tune on the harp.
He said, "I will come one day reciting poems."
There was so little opposition to his words
that what he said did indeed come true.

You are the soul and the Universe.   133
The world is beautiful and pleasant because of You.
This wound is the wound from Your spear
and that is wonderful.
Dirt in Your hand is a treasure trove of alchemy.
Everything unpleasant becomes pleasant
because of You.

Your eyes shed more blood than time.   134
Your eyelash is sharper than a spear.
You whispered a secret in my ear.
Say it loudly once more.
I seem to have a problem with my hearing.

135   There is no one like my Beloved among the Beauties.
      Unlike the Universe, He is not subject to destruction.
      He has no end.
      If a confused one utters a bunch of nonsense about this, say to him,
      "Say what you will. It doesn't matter.
      My Beloved is still the most beautiful One."

136   Now I know that Love cannot be separated from me.
      It has been bound to me.
      Its braided hairs are in my hand.
      Yesterday, I was drunk thanks to the glass.
      Today, the glass is drunk thanks to me.

There is no Beloved in the world as beautiful as You.   137
Nothing is better than seeing Your face.
You are my friend, my Beloved in both worlds.
Every beauty is a reflection of Your light.

   God forbid! I would never say,   138
"I am too tired to stay with you late into the night."
Neither would I say,
"Our cupbearer is without help."
But, sleepiness has made the mind
fall on the floor like a shadow.
It is too late now. Come back early in the morning.

139   The ground You step on brings happiness to my soul.
That ground turns into roses and jasmine.
Flowers and fruits grow well, too, on that ground.
How could I stop prostrating there?

140   If you want the Beloved to show His face to you,
turn inside.
Walk to the Essence and give up your flesh.
He is such an Essence
that He is surrounded by layers of curtains.
He is submerged into His own Being,
and both worlds are submerged within Him.

Beloved, the sun of Your face doesn't fit in the skies.   141
Your Beauty cannot be described with words.
Although Your Love is beyond the Universe,
it has made my heart its home.

Rise, because the One   142
who is the source of happiness has risen.
Rise, because the One
to whom everyone is indebted has risen.
Your Love has entered my soul.
Such Beauty is beyond life and this Universe.

143   Although steps are taken to progress in Love,
those steps are taken in a place beyond place.
You see so many beings in the house of illusions.
Look at them carefully.
If you rub your tired eyes,
you will see that the majority of them
don't even exist.

144   Step towards the Fountain's Water of Life.
Start turning like the sky
around that moon-faced Beloved.
The soul of the Universe is turning around Him.
That soul is caught in His rotation.

Step on the road which has no end.   145
Watching from a distance is not for a man.
Start the journey with the strength of the heart.
The body's strength is for animals.

Good or bad, apparent or hidden,   146
everything is under the command of God.
I strive with great effort, but fate tells me,
"There are things beyond your control."

147   There is a different air in the gathering of lovers,
a different drunkenness from Love's wine.
The knowledge you gain from a religious school
is one thing.
But Love is another, and it's entirely different.

148   There is a new life in death
for the man of faith and justice.
From death, peace and calm come to clean souls.
Death is reaching out to God,
not out to fear and cruelty.
The one who refuses to die with that death
will die every day.
That is the greatest of all troubles.

You have two hands, two feet, two eyes. That is true. 149
But, it would be a mistake
to count the heart and the Beloved as two.
Saying "Beloved" is only a pretext.
In fact, God is the Beloved.
Whoever says God is two is an impious infidel.

That splendid Beloved 150
who is on the other side of the curtain
said about me,
"He is no good, because opening up is not his habit."
But as soon as He saw me, He changed His words, saying
"You are Mine. Those words were not about you."

151   I don't yell and cry if the Beloved skins me,
      because that pain comes from Him.
      For me, everyone is my enemy. He is my only friend.
      It is not nice to complain to enemies about friends.

152   The Beloved is elegant. That is not His fault.
      He is beautiful and charming. That is not His fault.
      I wonder which fault they found in Him
      which caused them to run away.
      Maybe it is the fact that He is perfect.
      That is not His fault.

The One to whom our heart belongs is our Beloved. 153
Wherever lightning strikes,
sparks flash out from our jewels.
All gold carries the seal of, "Am I not your Lord?"[11]
It doesn't matter which mine that gold comes from.
It is our gold.

Your sorrow has made my heart wail and cry. 154
It has forced bloody tears from my eyes.
All life receives anguish and affliction because of it.
And because of it, I am about to die.
I am sorrowful, so that someday
I may go beyond Your sorrow.

---

[11] Quran 7:172.

155   O Beloved, my heart rejoices
      only when it remembers You.
      I swear to God it is not because of wine.
      My heart has thrown away the glass.
      It considers itself dead without You.
      That is justice for the one
      whose soul has run away from You.

156   When my heart sat down to drink,
      You came to my mind.
      My heart grabbed the glass from the cupbearer,
      broke it and began leaping with joy.
      It was neither drunk nor sober.
      The rumor spread that it had gone crazy-insane.

I have become crazy-insane. 157
It is not proper for me to sleep.
How could a crazy one know how to sleep?
"God never sleeps."[12]
His insane ones follow His example.
The crazy-insane ones
are the intimate companions of God.

Yesterday, the Beloved was so kind as to ask me, 158
"How can you live without Me?"
I answered, "By God, like a fish without water."
"That is your fault," He said, "so do not weep."

---

[12]Quran 2:255.

159 The one who was looking at us yesterday
     was either the soul of an angel
     or the spirit of a beautiful being.
     Anyone who lives without seeing His beautiful face
     is dead.
     Knowledge of anything without Him
     comes from total ignorance.

160 Any day I see You,
     I consider that day to be a Friday.
     My day today is better than yesterday
     because of Your grace.
     Even if thousands of worlds nursed a grudge against me,
     I would not care,
     as long as the Love of the Beloved is in my heart.

When weather frowns and clouds cry, 161
it is for the sake of the leaves, the fruits and flowers.
In order to let their children be happy and playful,
parents struggle and wear themselves out.

The tambourine is subjected to blows and beating. 162
That is why its sound lights up the Sema gathering.
The tambourine says, "Long life to the one who hits me!
Those rhythmic wounds nourish my heart."

163   I am drunk with the wine
which is from the glass engraved with Love.
I ride a horse whose reins are Love.
Falling in love with my moon-faced one is wonderful,
but I am a slave and servant of the One
who made a slave and servant of Love.

164   O confused heart, the way to the Beloved
is through your soul.
O one who has lost his way,
there is a road to the Beloved
which is both known and unknown.
Don't worry if your way is blocked
from all six directions.
There is a way right from the bottom of your heart.

An asset of wisdom is the secret of madness. 165
Love's insane one is the wisest man in the world.
If a man learns the heart's mysteries
through suffering,
he becomes a thousand times a stranger to himself.

My moon-faced one is the Sultan of beauty and charm. 166
This insane heart of mine is chained by His Love.
I shed my blood on the dust at His doorstep.
Yet, that dust is more valuable than my blood.

167   The hyacinth's beauty is nothing
compared to the beauty of your curls.
In the universe of beauty, there is nothing
like your flowing curls.
After seeing them, the hyacinth twisted, imitated,
and talked about them.
But, it could never reach their splendor.

168   My heart is Your student. It is learning Love.
Like the passing night,
it begs for help from the morning.
Wherever I go, the face of Love is facing me.
Like the oil in a lamp,
my heart faces the One who burns it.

I have told you hundreds of times, 169
when you meet someone who is drunk or sober,
don't be unruly.
Don't strike at every branch you see.
Still, you have given your heart to this and that,
decreasing the value of your beauty
and extinguishing the fire in my heart.

One cannot be a lover 170
unless he is as light and pleasant as a soul.
He is not a lover
if he doesn't turn around the Moon like a star.
Hear this from me, "Leaves don't move without a breeze."

171 Love came and broke my regret as if it were a bottle.
Who can repair a broken bottle except Love?
How can we escape
Love's constant breaking and repairing?

172 Love came and became the blood in my veins and skin.
It emptied me from my self,
filling me up with the Beloved.
Every part of my body is now occupied by the Beloved.
Only my name has been left to me.
He has become everything else.

Why is Your Love so wise, so supreme? 173
Why is Your compassion so tender?
If it is not pleasing, why do I love Love so much?
If it is so pleasing, why do I cry and wail?

It is Love which gives life to a body made of clay. 174
Why is this Love so sweet, so beautiful?
Is it inside or outside of my body?
Or, is it in the gaze of God's Shams of Tabriz?

175   All life long, the soul has been a slave and servant
of the One without self, without existence.
That is why it is so distinct
from the men and women of this world.
It is easy to take leave of the soul and this world.
But, it is very difficult to give up Your presence.

176   Reason came to advise the lovers.
It sat in the middle of the road
and stopped them one by one.
But, when it realized it couldn't find
a place in their minds,
it kissed their feet, then disappeared.

When the wind caresses those scattered hairs,   177
the moon is praying,
saying from the bottom of its heart,
"May your life be long."
O one who gives me advice,
if your heart were to taste the pleasure of my heart,
you would give that advice to yourself.

If you are still deceived by your lust,   178
your fancies and desires,
I tell you
that you will come and go in this world empty-handed.
If you get them under control,
you will know where you came from
and where you are going.

179   If I cry out with pain,
my wails are not enough for my Beloved.
If I become like dirt on the road,
it is not enough for my Sultan.
If I prostrate all night like a shadow adoring the Moon,
it is still not enough for my moon-faced Beloved.

180   If there is no fire in my heart, what is this smoke?
If aloe wood hasn't been burned, what is this smell?
Why do I exist if I am a non-existent lover?
Why does the moth enjoy burning
in the flame of the candle?

When you are with the Beloved, 181
you are in the orchard and garden of paradise.
When you are separated from the Beloved,
you are in hell with all of its tortures.
Love is eternal, but in this world, Love is concealed.
The strange thing is that Love undresses
the one who dresses Him.

If grief covers everywhere, everything, 182
the one who keeps holding on to Love becomes carefree.
Just look at the particle.
When it touched Love,
it turned into a shape which created universes.

183 If someone is ashamed and embarrassed
by this person or that one,
he buries their faults deep down under.
If he displays good and evil like a mirror,
his face, like a mirror, must be of polished iron.[13]

184 If there is no tambourine,
we have the ney which comes from His sugar reed.
And, His wine of Love is in our hands.
Isn't Kayqubad[14] in our ranks,
that Emperor known for
breaking through enemy lines?
And, isn't Solomon our secret advisor?

---

[13]In medieval Asia Minor, mirrors were made of polished metal.
[14]The Seljuk Sultan of Rum who reigned 1220-1237 CE.

No one could touch the curls of Your hair   185
without drinking wine from Your drunken eyes.
My enemies mock me day and night, saying,
"You get drunk and are unable to walk,
yet Your Beloved doesn't even hold your hand."

Everyone is crazy with some desire.   186
There is a yearning, a longing in everyone's head.
The pleasure which creates that yearning is obvious.
But, the source of the pleasure is obscure.

187   I said, "I will fly away from Your hand like a pigeon."
He answered, "If you do,
you deserve to be chained with My grief."
I said, "I have become helpless and humiliated
because of You."
He answered, "Your glory and honor
are a result
of that helplessness, those humiliations."

188   I said to the Beloved, "My eyes are the dust on Your path.
Don't make them cry
out of longing to see Your face."
He answered, "Isn't it enough
that being in the shadow of My kindness
gives you honor your whole life long?"

He said, "Come. Sema is reaching its peak." 189
I said. "This slave has a very high fever."
He said, "Even if you are dead,
you will come back to life.
The Jesus of our time is passionately working."

A head which is not under the foot of the lover 190
should perish,
and so should a heart
which has not been ship-wrecked
by the sorrow of Love.
There is no space for even a hair
between a lover and the Beloved.
So, even though I have become
as small as a piece of hair,
I still cannot fit there.

191   You aren't worth a penny
if you have a golden tongue,
but your affairs are in bad shape.
How can you start a long journey
with an unbroken, headstrong horse
which has less value than its saddle?

192   Some say,
"It is nice when Love and reason get together."
Others say, "When Love becomes a friend of the self,
stay away from that."
Both sayings are as good as gold.
But, my soul-sacrificing to Shams of Tabriz is best.

To be modest is not demeaning for a great man. 193
Acting like a child with children
comes from maturity.
If a father talks like a child, the wise man clearly knows
that the father is not a child.

My heart has left me and run to the One who, 194
unlike you and me,
has no self.
Sorrow is not pleasant, except when it comes from Him.
Although the Beloved is asking for my life,
I will delay a couple of days.
My life is worthless,
but His asking is my happiness.

195   Your kindness created such a universe,
      bestowing such a grace!
      It arranged its designs in such a pleasing way!
      A small piece was dropped into this ocean
      and a grain from Your granary
      was planted on this plain.

196   We are the lovers of Love. Love is our salvation.
      The soul is like Khidr.[15] Love is like the Water of Life.
      Alas to the one who is not decorated by the Sultan of Love.
      How could an animal know the soul's sugar?

---

[15] A legendary man who is said to have attained immortality by drinking from the Water of Life and who comes to help those in moments of extreme distress.

We are lovers of Love. Muslims are different. 197
We are small ants. Solomon is different.
Ask us about our pale faces and broken hearts.
Silk merchants are different.

You cannot control us with some old spell. 198
You cannot keep us in this suffocating place.
Once someone is chained to that long curly hair,
they cannot be chained to the inside of a house.

199   When my heart gave up the bait, be fair:
      it made a wise decision.
      When a lover gives up his heart,
      the Beloved holds his hand.
      When a lover throws out his soul and prostrates,
      he finds himself at the Beloved's feet.

200   Your drunken eyes made my eyes drunk.
      I became lost in Your hands.
      Please help me.
      Shake Your head to say, "yes,"
      if that head is still a lover
      which exists in this existence.

I am Yours. You have to take care of me   201
and make me happy,
because everyone in this town is talking about us.
No matter how Your heart treats mine,
whether You are harsh or kind, I can take it.

I am a mountain. I am echoing the Beloved.   202
I am a painting. That Beauty is my painter.
Do you think all these words I say belong to me?
No, they are the sound of the key turning in the lock.

203   I am the slave of a person who is happy
without "I" and "we."
I share the sorrow of One who suffers alone.
They ask me about favors from the Beloved.
I don't know of any, but His cruelty delights me.

204   On the way to Truth,
after sweeping the streets with his eyelashes,
Master Hallaj[16] used to say, "I am God."
After plunging into the Sea of Absence,
he found the pearl of "I am the Truth"
and drilled a hole in it.

---

[16]Hallaj Mansur, a famous Sufi martyred for his beliefs (858-922 CE).

Cry and a neighbor may hear you,   205
that neighbor who is the One so very close to you.
Although the nanny may act like she doesn't care,
a baby's cry softens the nanny's heart.
Keep crying. Crying is an asset of Love.

When that Beauty suddenly entered through my door,   206
He was drunk.
He sat, drinking ruby-colored wine.
I got lost looking at His beautiful hair.
My whole face turned into eyes,
and my eyes became hands.

207 Suddenly, a sugar cane sprouted up.
Suddenly, the Water of Life spouted out.
Suddenly, alms started flowing
from the Sultan of sultans.
So, pray for God's benediction
on the soul of Muhammad.

208 You must fulfill my desire.
You must please my heart,
because in this town, everyone is talking about us.
It doesn't matter if your heart is hard or tender.
You will come to me
like sweet water spouting out of hard rock.

I am not content being with You. 209
Yet, there is no chance of surviving without You.
My mind has become dizzy because of this situation,
and this is an incurable disease, not a situation.

An army could never be gathered 210
without the money and power of the Sultan.
Travel could never be secured
without the courage and desire of the guard of the road.
Only the one who is able to protect his pitcher
can carry it through the stony field.

211   Fate is not a slave to our selves
      which are being forged on this path of fire.
      Existence is the means to reach Absence.
      The One who cares for us is behind the curtain.
      In fact, we are not here.
      What appears is merely our shadow.

212   Look carefully.
      Every particle of the Earth and sky is as crazy as we are.
      Somber or cheerful, they all keep turning
      around the Sun of Absence.

Come to yourself. Be brave, O wounded heart.   213
Don't act as if you are estranged from Love.
Forget everything under the rule of reason.
Now is the time for exuberance and madness!

When our Beloved makes a soul merry,   214
that soul stays forever happy,
keeping forever a smile on its lips.
This dimension of the soul does not come from a lover.
It comes, and I say this quietly,
only from the Beloved.

215 Separation may break hope's back.
Sorrow may tie the hands of desire.
But, the heart of a drunken lover
never falls into desperation.
A committed heart always prevails.

216 Don't ever think that the dervish
who annihilates his self
is fed by illusions.
The imperial tent of his Beauty,
which is pitched beyond existence,
beyond the Universe,
is far better than existence,
far better than the Universe.

One who has attained the Truth knows well   217
that fate comes from His workshop.
Why blame the Earth and the stars?
They don't even control their own rotations.

The sober one is like a horse   218
which is worth less than its saddle.
It doesn't matter if he possesses gold
or dresses with gold.
The one who hasn't been to the tavern is not a man.
The tavern of Love is the foundation of true faith.

219 He is such a Beloved
that a rose and a thorn are the same for Him.
In His religion, the Quran and the Bible are the same.
Don't try to impress Him.
For Him, a fleet of horses and a lame donkey
are exactly the same.

220 He is devout and pious,
but blood-thirsty at the same time.
His thirst is the essence of abstinence.
When the Sun favors such a servant,
it is understandable that that servant
would be a night-riser.

Last year, nothing else was in my heart day or night   221
except goodness and kindness and virtue.
But this year, I am in such an indescribable shape!
And next year?
Woe to me and woe to goodness, kindness and virtue.

O one who criticizes my wine-drinking,   222
don't think that this wine is coming from grapes.
My exuberance is my wine. My heart is my glass.
My cupbearer is the One
who illuminates the darkness every morning.

223 O Beloved, Your face is an exquisite mirror to the soul.
I wish You would walk
into my morning thoughts and reflections,
rubbing Your feet across my face and eyes.
But, considering how flawed of body and sight I am,
I am afraid that my eyelashes might hurt You.

224 Learned men said different things about Absence.
Armed with all their ignorance,
they pierced the pearl of wisdom,
but were unable to understand
the secrets of the Universe.
First, they wise-acred.
Then, they fell on the ground and slept.

The Beloved's Water of Life is the cure for all diseases. 225
No thorn is left
on the Beloved's sapling rose of Union.
They say, "There is a window between hearts."
But, there are no windows if no walls remain.

O my soul, sugar is made carefully out of sugarcane. 226
Silk is made by silk worms out of mulberry leaves.
Be patient.
Unripe fruit is made into sweet paste only with time.

227 Nothing is left of the army of my patience except a flag.
Nothing is left of my belongings except sorrow.
That distant Beloved is still amorously playful.
He still bestows His breath.
Yet, not much more than one breath is left for me.

228 No ill temper is left thanks to Your good nature.
No sorrow or trouble about more or less remains.
Troops of Your majesty have conquered the Universe.
All have become sultans, and no poor ones remain.

You are being followed closely day and night.   229
You can't see the hunter, but you will be cut down.
You will be cut off from everyone and everything,
including your self.
If you don't go along,
you will be violently dragged away.

The eyes whose hearts   230
were burned out by the fire of fall
have been opened again by the kindness of spring.
New dresses have been made for them.
They have been taught new charms
and new endearing and amorous behaviors.

231 For a lover, a scholar who searches for Truth
behind this door
is like a piece of straw.
The one who becomes master of his own heart
is in the company of the Sultan of sultans.
All the rest are expenses required for the journey.

232 The ones who live in the quarter of lovers
are active until the day of Resurrection.
Their hearts are full of joy.
Some people are ready to sacrifice themselves
to the world.
But, others are already free
from both the self and the world.

When people come from non-being,   233
they are drunk with the words,
"Am I not Your Lord?"[17]
Their souls worship Love.
But, once they put their heads on the feet of their souls,
they begin times full of troubles.

One who is like pure, clear water   234
flows like wine through the minds and souls of people.
I have given up everything, freed myself from desires,
lain down and stretched out my legs.
That is what one does
when one is traveling on a boat on this river.

---

[17]Quran 7:172.

235 Those who abandon good friends
have listened to fanciful stories.
They feel the breath of the robbers on the road
and stumble like lame goats,
becoming the prey of hungry wolves.

236 The ones who reach this path and stay on it
learn Your secrets one by one.
And, out of kindness,
they don't tear away the curtains of others.
While traveling through this world,
they are as quiet and tolerant as passing time.

The beguiling beauty of the idol who seized my heart   237
took me to the tavern of idols.
Those idols appear like pious souls.
But actually, they are blood-thirsty brigands.

When they arranged and appraised the world,   238
they put a different seal on the gold of lovers.
You will never understand this sealing business
with your mind.
It was performed outside of that realm.

239 When fate gives knowledge and wisdom to someone,
it cuts his sustenance and throws him into poverty.
It fills the ignorant one with wealth instead of wisdom
and turns him into a storehouse or granary.

240 Pay no attention to a person's skill and knowledge.
Instead, look to see if he is keeping the promise
which he made in Eternity.
Is he loyal?
If he is, praise him, because he is better
than any other character you have found so far.

Sit next to God's lovers. 241
They will dispel your confusion
and clear away the smoke of your sorrow.
Don't ever think badly of them,
because they will know your thoughts
before you even think them.

A human is made by mixing opposite materials. 242
His shape and features are drawn on the table of sorrow.
Sometimes he is an angel,
sometimes a devil
and sometimes a beast.
What is this mysterious magic
which mixes everything together?

243   O Love, paris[18] know You and so do humans.
       They know You better than the seal of Solomon.
       They think You are the soul of the body of the world.
       Yet no one knows how I live with You
       except the birds.

244   O Love, all souls are the images of Your Soul.
       You are the source of all beauty and pleasure.
       O Love, all gold is from Your mine.
       All are naked,
       while You are covered with beautiful garments.

---

[18] In Persian mythology, mischievous winged spirits famous for their beauty.

O Water of Life, whoever tastes Your wine of Love   245
adds Life to his life.
Death came and sniffed me,
but it caught Your scent, and ever since then,
it has left me alone.

O Love, who are You?   246
You are the whole. You are everything.
Everything belongs to You.
All gold comes from Your mine.
You fill people with sorrow and longing,
so they become scattered and confused.
O Love, You are the mother.
All of humanity are Your children.

247   O heart, you go nowhere on this road
with talk and gossip.
You cannot reach the Beloved
unless you pass through the door of Absence.
O heart, you must take to the air where His birds fly.
Otherwise, they will not grant you wings.

248   O Love, You are the meaning of the verse,
"My punishment is terrible indeed."[19]
Your lover has been martyred
by the blow of Your sword.
It is night. Everyone is asleep now.
But, where is my sleep?
Perhaps some wolves have devoured it.

---

[19] Quran 14:7.

He came again.   249
He showed His curly hair again.
He displayed that cruelty,
that evil, that blaming again.
That Moon who made the flag of Venus
turn upside down
came again with the imperial drum and banner.
Be loyal! Be strong! Be unwavering!

Some are brave, like Haydar-e Karrar.[20]   250
Others are easily wounded,
wounded by even a heron.
Your Love says,
"I want only strong lovers, the most perfect ones
to walk on this way."
You say,
"But, there are so many broken hearts on this road."

---

[20] Ali, a cousin of the Prophet Muhammad, known for his courage in battle and called "the Boldly Attacking Lion."

251   Once I caught Your fragrance,
      I was forced to go Your way.
      My color and scent were stolen by Yours.
      I was annihilated in the end,
      so nothing was left of me.
      Not even a hint of scent remained.

252   Water washed away all of my poetry.
      All of my belongings were carried away by the flood.
      My goodness and badness, my worship and devotion
      were given to the moonlight,
      and the moonlight took them away.

They will not allow you to go inside of you   253
as long as you stay with your self.
Only if you annihilate your self
will they keep you in their eyes and hearts.
Only if you give up both worlds
will they stamp you with the seal of Absence.

Don't travel alone on this road.   254
This road is full of brigands.
You are only one and the enemies are many,
and what's worse, you think they are your friends.
In this world, there are many naive ones like you.

255   Gamble with your life. Take every chance you can.
You won't reach His Union by talking.
They don't serve milk to drunks
from the cup of religious law.
In the place where wine is served,
they pour it only to those
who have undressed from the self.
Not even a drop is given to those who worship themselves.

256   Don't go to any place
except the place of lovers and drunks.
Don't let your heart get involved with bad company.
Everyone tries to pull you to their side,
the raven to ruin, the parrot to sugar.

Your words made me speechless.   257
Your sweetness made me soft and idle.
I ran from Your traps to the house of my heart.
But, the house of my heart became the trap for me.

There is no room for the conceited at the tavern.   258
Only the respectful and honest are allowed.
You must gamble once you get in.
You may be checkmated.
You may lose.
You may win.

259 So many lovers make the journey to Your door.
Their numbers are always increasing.
They shed bloody tears, but then they keep traveling.
I stay on forever like the dust on Your door step,
while others come and go like the wind.

260 When the army of Love wants to shed blood,
they sharpen their swords by cutting off pieces of me.
I am drowning in this heart
which is as deep as the sea,
so please tell my friends
to be careful and not come near.

I am tied up with that hair full of knots and curls. 261
I am wailing to get to those sugar lips.
O beauty whose promise of union
seems to be worth nothing,
how long will the sorrow of our separation last?

I will place the sorrow of Love in my heart. 262
I will make my soul the target of the arrows of trouble.
If any part of my life is devoid of Your Love,
I will sacrifice that part with the blood of my heart.

263 I went to the house of that charming Beauty
who welcomed me with smiles and laughter.
He pressed me to His chest,
embracing me with a sweetness like sugar, saying,
"O lover, O learned one, O sage!"

264 This day is the day of joy. Why should we be sad?
Today, we should drink wine from the cup of loyalty.
How long will we expect our sustenance
to be from the bread-maker, the water-carrier?
This is the time to be eating and drinking
from the hand of God.

My heart must sacrifice thousands of souls   265
as a sign of gratitude
for the day it was filled with the sorrow of the Beloved.
O chosen one on the way of Love,
you won't get help and guidance from the Beauties
unless you are grateful.

Don't ever say,   266
"No one walks toward the Truth nowadays.
No one is like Jesus, like a concealed saint in our time."
Since you are not intimate
with the secrets of the path,
you are assuming that everyone else is ignorant, too.

267   One should drink poison
      from the hand of that silver-bodied Beauty.
      One should taste His harsh words as if they were sugar.
      The Beloved is the taste and salt of everything.
      One could eat one's own liver with that salt.

268   When trees are covered
      with their spring-colored flowers,
      those Jacobs are seeing their Josephs.
      Those trees dressed in black
      for the long winter days.
      After grieving, now they can smile.

The tree branches are covered with fresh flowers. 269
They had lost all their leaves,
but they had also seen pearls in their hearts,
so they stayed standing up.
They didn't lose hope. They didn't bend.

Night has come. It is time for people to fall asleep 270
like the fish which plunges back into the water.
In the morning, most will follow the steps of reason.
Only a few will walk towards the One
who created reason.

271 Since you are not a peacock,
who would want to admire your beauty?
Since you are not a phoenix,
who would call your name when you were absent?
Since you are not a royal falcon,
who would expect a piece of your prey?
So, what kind of bird are you,
and how could they eat you?

272 The world is charmed by His attributes.
Everything, everyone seems to exist.
But, they are all annihilated in front of Him,
and only the one who can lift the curtain of mortality
may reach the Essence behind His attributes.

Lovers may give up both worlds   273
in one moment.
They may sacrifice a hundred years of life
in one moment.
They go through thousands of stages
after getting one moment of that fragrance.
They sacrifice thousands of their souls
to please just one Heart.

Your Love turns every place of worship into a tavern.   274
Your Love sets a bazaar of idols aflame.
The hands of Your sorrow, like thieves,
reach out everywhere and grab us in both worlds.

275 There is a group of people
who stay in Your tavern all the time.
There are holy rascals among them.
How many? Who knows?
They don't like to be sober – ever.
They laugh at the good and bad of this world
all the time.

276 If you start the journey,
they will open the road for you.
If you annihilate yourself,
they will carry you to Absence.
Humble yourself,
and they will grow you greater than the Universe.
Become nothing, and they will show You without you.

If sharks infested all the seas,   277
if tigers covered all the plains,
if the greediest were satisfied by wealth,
lovers would still keep their eyes fixed
on the face of the Beloved.

I said, "O Beloved, You are a soul,   278
and to bid farewell to a soul is impossible."
He answered, "One cannot know the soul
in the way one knows the body."
I said, "You are a sea of generosity."
He answered, "Be silent. Love is not given for free.
It is a pearl of the Sea, not a stone."

279   Where is that beautiful Joseph,
the one for whom the whole Universe
has become Jacob?
Where is the patience
which has allowed lovers to become Job?
When a broken heart dances in the gathering of souls,
it leaves traces of blood wherever it steps.

280   Who said that that immortal spirit has died?
Who said that the Sun of hope has gone out?
It is the enemy of evidence
who has climbed up on the roof,
closed his eyes and said, "The Sun has died."

Who said that the soul which created Love is dead?   281
Who said that the Archangel Gabriel
has been killed with a sharp dagger?
The one who himself died as an obstinate devil
has been alleging that the Sun of Tabriz has died.

They brought us here from the tavern of Eternity.   282
That drunk donkey was brought here
to have drunken fights.
But, we have nothing to do
with such fighting, such disputing.
They mixed us with milk and honey.

283   They brought us here, drunk and exuberant,
      from the tavern of "Am I not your Lord?"[21]
      We came from Absence to existence.
      They will pull us back again to that tavern.

284   We are longing for Him
      and others are longing for Him, too.
      We will see who will be so blessed
      as to reach His Union.
      His sorrow has replaced both mind and manners
      with playing and smiling.

---

[21]Quran 7:172.

I am a slave and servant of those people 285
who know themselves.
They save their souls from mistakes every second.
They write a book about their Essence and attributes
and name that book, "I am the Truth."

I am tired of sitting on the bench of the Universe 286
because of all the people of ill repute
and all of their bickering.
From first to last
they do nothing but boast and talk nonsense.
At my appointed time, I will welcome death.

287   I will not be like those people
who talk about purity and goodness.
I will not drink their wine.
As long as I have strength in my legs,
I will make proclamations loudly and clearly
until the good names of those people are ruined.

288   Wherever they have sown the seeds of loyalty
in this world,
they have harvested those seeds
from our threshing floor.
Wherever a ney and tambourine are played,
that is our joy, even if they think it is their own.

They beat the drum of Your Love at night, announcing,   289
"The time for His Love has come!"
My body becomes soul after the humdrum of the day.
Love has so many daughters
hidden behind the dress of night.
They will pull sorrow's beard and mustache
if sorrow comes.

Only sultans know the secret of spring.   290
Animals are content to eat grass and chew thorns.
If there is one who cannot see
the power of creation, that divine art,
even if he is old, consider him immature.
The rose garden is adorned for lovers,
not for immature ones.

291   You are nothing.
But, your nothingness is better than existence.
You are lost in losses.
But, your loss is better than gain.
You say, "I have nothing but a handful of dust."
But, the sky is envious of that dust.

292   O One who fills the Earth with honey and sugar!
O One who brings death to conquerors!
Please, come with roses and laurels!
I hear how my Beloved is calling me loudly,
"O lover, O loyal friend, O learned one!"

O pious ones, keep praying toward the niche. 293
Time is passing, and there is a long way ahead.
Hurry up.
O searchers for the Truth at the tavern,
you are drowning.
Hundreds of caravans have passed,
yet you are still sleeping.

O Beloved, the sea boils with passion 294
because of Your Love.
The clouds rain pearls at Your feet.
Lightning strikes the Earth
and smoke ascends to the sky
all because of Your Love.

295 O Beloved, my face gains beauty
     from Your Beauty!
     Your beautiful image is always in my eyes!
     My heart is filled with Your grace and mercy.
     There is a different Beauty today,
     a different maturity in our Sema.

296 There is a flame of youth in Your Love.
     The peerless beauty of Your soul appears in my heart.
     O Beloved, if You want to kill me, I am all Yours!
     New life comes from being killed by the Beloved.

If messengers didn't bring help from Love, 297
how could the smart one and the fool sustain themselves?
Your Love is like a tangled silk ball,
not for the impatient to untie.

Love's fire warms cold hearts and melts stones. 298
Forgive lovers for their sins, O friend!
A man becomes shameless
when he drinks Love's wine.

299   There is One
whom I would love to give up my life for
just so I could be together with Him.
A piece of His hair is worth the whole gold mine.
But, there is another one whom I don't wish
to be talking with,
because avoiding him is worth
the wealth of the whole world.

300   Do not change the melody of the heart
so that the pleasure of that melody
will not disappear.
Do not look at anything except the heart
so that its sweetness will not disappear.
Your ecstasy is like paradise,
so do not give up your drunkenness.
Stay on the journey
so that that paradise will not disappear.

Your grace gives hope to everyone.   301
Your favor is eternal fortune.
Particles which receive Your grace
for the length of a breath
glow brighter than a thousands suns.

You remember the Creator of the Universe   302
when you are in trouble.
If you call Him deep down in your heart and soul,
He will come to help.
But, if you are not sincere in your plea,
you will get nothing.

303   Your drunken beauty could charm
      even a granite stone,
      bringing it back to life and making it like a beloved.
      When your love displays like a drunk's,
      your curls are revealed,
      and that would make even Luqman[22] insane.

304   Get some sparks from the Beloved's fire
      and burn out this fodder.
      Since His sorrow's hand
      has already grabbed the ney of your heart,
      start playing this tambourine.

---

[22]Known as Luqman the Wise. The thirty-first sura [chapter] of the Quran is named after him.

O heart, no harm will come to you from death. 305
How can you become lifeless
once you become pure soul?
First, you came from the sky to the Earth.
In the end, you will ascend back to the sky.

It is too bad that your character 306
cannot enlighten anyone.
You have done nothing
except hurt and break hearts.
I have given you my heart, my life, my eyes,
and you have just taken them all!
What can I do when faced with your bad fortune?

307   Now that the beauty of your face
has caught the soul of the world,
what is the use of hiding in the house?
Didn't you know that when you became
like the Moon grown full,
everyone would be pointing their finger at you?

308   The One who commands the skies
knows all of your secrets.
He knows you hair by hair and vein by vein.
You might be able to deceive people with your lies.
But, how can you deceive Him?
He knows everything, detail by minuscule detail.

Sema was full of joy and pleasure today.   309
All the worlds spun around me in endless celebration.
My soul lost its grip. My body shed its fatigue.
Hearing the clap of your hands
and the beat of your tambourine,
my heart discarded its old belt,
and I floated up to the heavens.

Today is a nice day for that lover.   310
He has offered his life
at the feet of that Beauty's Sultan.
He has turned into a drunken nightingale
with the fire of separation in his heart.
He stays in that beauteous rose garden day and night.

311   Today is a nice day, a happy and cheerful one.
He who has soul drinks wine from the glass of eternity.
His heart swims in the Water of Life.
The one who carries the fire of Love in his heart
doesn't care what happens around him.

312   Birds have never heard the secrets of my words.
And, some things I have said may never be heard,
even by Solomon.
All secrets are apparent to lovers behind the curtain.
But, that secret of my words
is not known even to the soul.

Could my heart remain where You are now? 313
Wherever the glow of Your face shines,
the path of the heart is clear.
You said, "I need a reasonable person as a friend."
But, after seeing You,
how could reason remain in anyone?

Fasting in Ramadan turns your body into gold. 314
It grinds your existence to make salve for your eyes.
When you break fasting,
every bite becomes a pearl of meaning.
Your patience in fasting opens the eye of your heart.

315 If there would be more sorrow and mourning
in the houses of the disloyal ones,
then the number of disloyal ones
would be diminished in this world.
As you can see,
no one looks after me except loyal sorrow.
Thousands of thanks and praises to that sorrow!

316 Your beautiful face changes my night into day.
The sighs made for the sake of Your curly locks
are guides on the road.
Hundreds of blind ones have benefited
in Your village of sorrow.
Perhaps some night the wounded and scarred ones
will benefit, too.

The heart will not bother with this temporary world   317
once it sees the face of that secret, hidden Beauty.
At the time of my death,
I do not want my eyes looking at my soul.
I want them fixed instead on the face of that Beloved.

The peace of my soul   318
keeps turning around my heart and my soul.
I grow like a tree from the earthly ground of my body
because the Water of Life is turning around me.

319 When God ties off the belly-button of someone,
that person hears the cry of lovers.
He runs away from the trap of desires.
He flies to the place where other birds never fly.

320 When a person who is anxious to be rid of shame
breaks his old ties and falls into Love,
when that person undresses
like peeled garlic from earthly habits,
he doesn't give the head of an onion
for the whole entire world.

My God, the thing this poor soul wants from You   321
is something not even sultans would dare ask for.
Every particle is happy in the sunshine,
but every particle is still distant from Your Sun.
Your Sun is the thing this penniless beggar wants.
He wants Your entire Sun.

It would be easier to die by your hand   322
if you were to turn your eyes away from me.
But, I do have one worry:
Who will console you
when your eyes are wet with mourning for me?

323   What medicine could a doctor give to the Beauty
who is able to charm him,
able to take away his heart?
If that Beauty were to show him
even a small sign of His Beauty,
by God, the doctor would need a doctor for himself!

324   The day my soul starts its journey to the sky
is the day when every cell in my body
will mix with dirt.
If You write, "Rise up,"
with Your finger on that dirt,
life will return to me,
and I will jump from that grave.

The particle which stays   325
in the sole company of Your Sun
gains value and never falls victim to expectations.
Is there any head into which Your Love has fallen
which doesn't sway like the branch of a willow tree
with the breeze of Love?

What is this thing which sees both inside and out,   326
looking at insane lovers in such an artful way?
Look at those eyes, how they see.
Who or what is it
looking out from those eyes?

327   Friends should get together on gray, rainy days,
      because a friend refreshes a friend.
      It's just like a springtime rose garden
      where every rose beautifies the others in that garden.

328   When Love fights with my heart,
      my soul gets scared and runs barefoot out of sight.
      I am a lover. You are crazy if you think I am wise.
      Wise is the one who stays away from me.

The day my soul put on the body's cloak,   329
the Sea of Kindness was raised by Your grace.
The flute of my heart became exuberant
after drinking wine from Your lips for the first time.

One who validates me   330
is treating me like I am one of those little dolls
for sale in the bazaar.
I am tired of this.
I am not for sale.
I am a slave of the one who rejects me.

331   The one who threw me into the fire of Love
dropped hundreds of sparks on my tongue.
When the flames had covered me in all six directions,
I sighed only, "Ah."
He immediately closed my mouth.

332   The one who has half a loaf of bread
and a small place to stay,
the one who asks for nothing
and who is asked for nothing,
that one is the happiest,
because he lives with Your joy
and has the best of both worlds.

When someone who comes from this mud   333
finds a beloved who also comes from mud,
he calms down and becomes happy for awhile.
Rare is the one who comes from this mud,
but goes beyond it,
beyond gardens and rivers and palaces.
He finds a priceless pearl,
a Divine Beloved like You.

Anyone who tries to see the Beloved   334
with the eyes of his head
resembles an infidel who is looking at a true believer.
Don't try to see an awakened lover with your sleepy eyes,
because those eyes cannot see secrets.

335 The charm of Your moon-face pulls me into the sky.
Your running water turns me like a wheel.
I will keep turning like a water mill
as long as the river of Love flows.
So many tulips smile, so many roses bloom
on the banks of that river.

336 The ground you step upon rejoices.
It becomes pregnant with pleasure
and brings hundreds of buds to life.
Seeing that, the stars in the sky
scream and applaud with joy,
and the Moon glances at the stars with amazement.

O swaying cypress, 337
may the cold winds of autumn never harm you.
O eye of the Universe,
may evil's eye never cast a glance at you.
You are the soul of the Earth and the sky.
May nothing touch your soul
except peace and comfort.

O my friend, would an unfortunate remark 338
make a good man kill his friend,
especially when that friend is the kind
who shares his troubles?
If you don't think I am your friend, go ahead.
Consider me to be your enemy.
Even so, how can you kill your enemy
with such harshness?

339   O Sun, rise so particles may start dancing.
Soul, be happy. Start dancing without head or feet.
There is One around whom the sky turns.
Where is He dancing?
Come close. I will whisper it into your ear.

340   O One who relieves my troubles!
Your grace is making cypresses
and rose gardens drunk!
The rose is drunk. Its thorns are deadly drunk!
Pour us all one more glass,
so we can join in Your drunken stream.

This Love sits next to warriors.   341
It is such a gazelle that it stays in the company of lions.
The House of Love has flourished eternally.
Do you think it will be ruined without you?

Whenever my heart has started talking,   342
it has always been disgraced and criticized
by the people who don't know Love.
O Beloved, my heart remembers
Your beautiful face so deeply
that Your image appears in it
with my every breath.

343   May the splendors of Selâhaddin[23] be kindled!
May they be poured into the eyes and souls of lovers!
May every soul which has become refined
and gone beyond refinement
be mixed with the dust of Selâhaddin!

344   This solitude is better than the company of thousands.
This freedom is sweeter than owning the entire world.
Being in God's vicinity for even a short time
is worth more than the soul,
more than the Universe,
more than the all of everything.

---

[23]This quatrain was most likely said after the death of Selâhaddin Zerkûbî, the goldsmith, Rumi's confidant after the disappearance of Shams.

When Your Love touches someone, 345
trouble starts pouring immediately on his head.
As soon as Mansur[24] revealed
only a small secret of Love,
he was hanged by the rope of envy.

This helpless, broken-hearted lover 346
has come back once again.
He went away on his feet,
but has come back upside down.
Consumed in longing for You,
he had left this poor world
and the narrowness of its humanity
in search of the land of sweetness and perfection.

---

[24]Hallaj Mansur, a famous Sufi martyred for his beliefs (858-922 CE).

347   The one who can see Your beautiful face
doesn't think about gardens and meadows.
The lover who has been illuminated by Your Love
doesn't think about lamps and candles.
They say,
"Sleep is the nourishment for reason and the mind."
Have you ever seen a lover
who thinks about reason and the mind?

348   Could the moon say, "I am as bright as He is?"
Never.
Could my lost heart claim to be a guide?
Never.
O Qibla of souls, could a soul break Your heart
and make You cry for someone?
Never.

One who passes by my grave becomes drunk.   349
If he stands there, he remains drunk for eternity.
If he dives into the sea, the sea becomes drunk.
If he goes into the ground,
his gravestone becomes drunk.
Drunk,
drunk,
drunk.

When He is passing me by,   350
the Beloved turns His head toward the ground.
He wants me to envy that ground, and I do.
It would be so nice to be the dirt in front of Him,
because being that dirt, He might look at me.

351 What would be the use
of lightning striking from the clouds of that world,
if no one were here to be burned?
There must be at least one loving heart in this world
for God's lightning to set it swiftly alight.

352 While I was reciting a poem,
my Beauty appeared offended.
He asked, "Are you measuring Me
by the meter of a poem?"
I answered, "Tell me, why do You want to ruin my poem?"
He said, "How can I fit into a poem?"

Hear this if you can: 353
"One has to go beyond oneself to reach Him."
When you do arrive in the world of Absence,
don't talk.
Ecstasy is the language there, not words.

Exuberant people smell like roses. 354
Obstinate ones resemble thorns.
A thorn is not thrown into the fire
just because of its proximity to the rose.
But, the rose remains in the fire
because of its proximity to the thorn.

355   May you always be happy and smiling.
May lovers' hearts and souls always be cheerful because of you.
May that one who doesn't rejoice when seeing you be sorry, befuddled and wretched.

356   I am sick from the trials of Love.
I have been tested mightily by grief.
But, this sorrow and longing rejuvenate me.
It is strange, but when I am sick with this illness, grief alone nourishes me.
Everything else only harms me.

My heart would not have turned to the Cave[25]   357
without Your friendship.
Sorrow is a pleasure when it comes from You.
Things become worthless in excess.
But, the more of it there is,
the more precious Your sorrow becomes.

Without the pure water from the Sea of Love,   358
our pearl would turn into stone.
If there were no world to be found inside of our soul,
our soul and that world would shrink and confine us.
Pain from the Beloved polishes your heart and soul.
Hold fast to it and it will clean away
all of your dirt and rust.

---

[25]Friends of the Cave. Quran 9:40.

359 There would be no joy or happiness without Love,
no beauty, no harmony in existence.
Even if hundreds of raindrops fell
from the clouds to the sea,
none would conceive a pearl without Love.

360 Forgive this slave who is sleepless.
Forgive this thirst for which there is no water.
Forgive,
because he who does not forgive
will receive no rewards from God.

Union with God cannot be achieved 361
until a person completely annihilates his self.
Such a Union is not the merging of two to make one.
Union is one's total annihilation.
Absurdity doesn't turn falsehood into Truth.
Only a fool says, "Everything is God."

O Beloved, when Your Love flared up in my heart, 362
everything else was burned to ashes.
My heart put my mind, books and lessons on a shelf
and replaced them all with poetry.

363 Not before the minarets and mosques come down
     will the dervish's affairs be settled.
     Not before faith becomes heresy
     and heresy becomes faith
     will the dervish become a true lover.

364 My heart has suffered so much
     since falling into sorrow, into longing for Your Love.
     Although my heart has been
     in this sort of trouble before,
     it has never before done such grieving and wailing.

Once the soul enters the body,   365
its neighbors become water and fire, air and earth.
A good grape shares its color with the bad ones.
May God give no one bad neighbors!

Once my soul turned its face to the Essence   366
and gave up whys and whats and hows,
it started seeing Eternity.
The secret of Love and the meaning of creation,
which had been concealed for so long,
appeared from behind thousands of curtains.

367   How could a soul who thinks about You disappear?
The waning moon does become a thin sliver.
But, that is just one step on its journey
to becoming a full moon.

368   It is heresy not to get excited
in front of Beauty such as Yours.
A mind which sees You
but remains in its head
is like a snake whose head should be crushed.

There are thousands of spells in your eyes. 369
Hundreds of thousands of souls
have been caught there.
Your hair is the darkness of heresy.
Your faith, like a moon's face,
appears brighter when framed by that heresy.

O Beloved, 370
You kill thousands of beauties with one look.
People die screaming if they get
the slightest glance from You.
The sultans of our time
execute their enemies on the gallows.
But, You have no need for gallows
because of Your narcissus eyes.

371   Don't, out of envy, crack a walnut
while its kernel is still soft and sweet
or crack a shell which contains a small pearl.
And, if you do crack one, remember:
there are thousands more just like it.

372   An eye which gazes upon that rose, that tulip
fills the whirling sky with wails and cries.
The intoxication you get from a one-year-old Love
you could never get from a thousand-years-old wine.

When every day infamy spreads over an entire age, 373
the one who becomes famous is not a courageous man.
If you are looking for a pearl, dive deep into the ocean.
Do not bother with the foam on the shore.

When the image of Your face returns, 374
my poor heart will also return to its place.
If my life were to come to its end
and I had only one breath left,
if then You came back,
everything which has passed would return.

375　　When the musician combined the minor mode
　　　　with the melody of Iraq,[26]
　　　　my heart let go of my mind
　　　　and freed itself from reason and the body.
　　　　"I am like fire," it said. "I rise up like smoke
　　　　as your breath increases my flame."

376　　When the dawn of God's Love breaks,
　　　　souls leave their bodies and fly.
　　　　The lover reaches a place
　　　　where he can see the Beloved without eyes.

---

[26]Modes of traditional Persian music.

When my eyes rested upon Your cheeks of silver, 377
my soul became like the ring of the letter mim,[27]
attaching itself to Your ruby lips.
Like Nimrod,[28] my heart disappeared
in the smoke created by the fire of Abraham's longing.

My heart will never stop watching Your face. 378
Nor will it ever give up Your favors.
Even thorns on my grave
will keep longing for You,
for You!

---

[27] A letter in the Arabic alphabet.
[28] The tyrannical king responsible for building the Tower of Babel. According to legend, Nimrod assembled an army to challenge Abraham, but Abraham produced an army of gnats. One entered Nimrod's ear and drove him out of his mind.

379   Blood boils in the hearts of lovers like a great river.
       Lovers are like foam, spinning over the whirling blood.
       Your body is a millstone. Love is the water.
       Without that water, how could the millstone turn?

380   I want my heart to be bloodied with Your sorrow.
       Please let me receive Your sorrow
       with elegance and grace.
       O heart, only a foolish heart is without His sorrow.
       Do not trust your vision
       until your sorrow becomes Him.

The Sun, serving You at Your temple,   381
dies in front of You.
Likewise, the pale-faced Moon, its heart broken,
dies in front of You.
Both that tall cypress and that full-blooming rose
have fallen on the ground, dying in front of You.
This bloodied and pierced heart
has also fallen on the ground, dying in front of You.

How could the sun ever equal the beauty of Your face?   382
How could even the fastest wind
ever touch a thread of Your hair?
Even reason, that king of the city of existence,
becomes crazy when he reaches Your town.

383   The sun doesn't stay at home,
but goes around the entire world,
never stopping in any corner.
Its light fills the sky, telling us,
"Our Creator never makes a mistake."

384   For anyone who has a heart in his chest,
life is difficult without Your Love.
Call crazy anyone who can keep his mind
after seeing Your flowing curls.

Once he is annihilated, 385
the one whose heart is tangled up with Your hair
reaches Essence.
You keep ordering,
"Drink wine, but don't get drunk."
How could someone drink wine without getting drunk?

If the sea cannot satisfy my thirst, 386
what could a stream do?
If I cannot go to the rose garden to smell roses,
what could that scent do?
If my Beloved is gone and neglects me,
but my patience remains,
let us see what my patience can do.

387   Don't search for a pearl in this muddy river.
      Dive to the bottom of the Ocean of Truth.
      The only one who deserves such a pearl
      is the one who finds it in that Ocean
      and reemerges still thirsty,
      but not for the river of life.

388   Come to the garden
      and watch the ones dressed in green.
      Look at the stores.
      Roses are being sold on every corner.
      A smiling rose tells a nightingale,
      "Be silent. Think about those
      who become eternally silent."

The dervish reveals the world's secrets every moment   389
and offers splendor for free.
The dervish is not one who begs for bread.
He is the one who donates soul.

There are thousands of moon-faced beauties   390
in the garden,
roses and violets offering beautiful scents,
water cascading along in the creek.
These are all pretext.
In fact, all are Him.

391　If hell were the only place where I could touch Your hair,
I would feel sorry for those in heaven.
If they called me to the fields of paradise,
but without You,
that endless plain would feel far too narrow to me.

392　In Love, no one is low, no one is high.
Neither sobriety nor drunkenness exist in Love.
There is no protector, no sheikh, no disciple in Love,
only poverty.
Poor wandering dervishes are in Love.

If you are in Love, but still calm,   393
what are you doing among lovers?
Be sharp like a thorn,
so the Beloved who resembles the rose
will be pressing you into His heart
and pulling you close to His side.

One who wishes to reach his destination on this journey   394
has to give up this world.
He also must take care of his gaze:
everything in this world is a manifestation
of His magnificence,
but one has to be able to see.

395   What is the use of advice
      when it comes to my Love for You?
      I have taken poison. What is the use of sugar?
      "Tie up his feet," they say about me.
      It is my heart which is crazy,
      so what is the use of tying up my feet?

396   Don't worry. The Heart-opener has suddenly come.
      The One who cheers hearts
      with beautiful melodies has come.
      He has broken the wings of sorrow
      as if they were the wings of a fly.
      He is saying, "That bird of fortune, the Simurgh,[29]
      has flown here from the Qaf[30] mountain!"

---

[29] A magical, legendary bird in Persian mythology, often equated with the phoenix.
[30] A legendary mountain surrounding the Earth. Where the Simurgh lives.

My heart lives by Your desire.   397
Its life and death depend on You.
Because of You, it feels and speaks.
It says, "La hawla,"[31]
every time it is frustrated by Love.
But, what is the use of La hawla
when it comes to Love?

The generosity of Your hand is so great   398
that it makes the clouds ashamed.
That same hand holds the steel sword in war.
The sun is ashamed in the morning
when it draws its sword of light
in front of Yours.

---

[31]"La hawla va la kuwwata illa billah." Praise and submission. "There is no strength or power but in God." Mentioned by a Muslim when facing a calamity or situation he cannot control. A variant can be found in Quran 18:39.

399   Last night, my heart and my adversary in Love
      were in the same place.
      They neither slept nor rested from dusk until dawn.
      As soon as morning came,
      with pale faces and sleepy eyes,
      they prepared for Your arrival, O perfect One.

400   Everything my heart says openly or secretly
      is about those curls
      which smell of musk and scatter ambergris.
      My heart is exuberant, those curls disorderly.
      That is why this exuberant one's words are so confused.

My heart ran hard after that Beloved, 401
but it was impossible to catch Him.
It gambled everything it had and lost.
Tired and frustrated,
it took refuge in a corner of my chest.
Not even my cunning had helped.

Last night, the Beloved was like a moon in the sky. 402
No, no, He was more beautiful than that,
more beautiful than the Sun,
more beautiful than anything I could ever imagine.
He was so beautiful
that His Beauty was indescribable,
and even beyond my ability to know.

403 Yesterday, this slave was the moon of the soul.
In his search for proofs and explanations,
he asked a difficult question.
No answer came.
But, his question disappeared.

404 Do good.
Time recognizes goodness.
It never forgets its value.
Everyone passes through this world,
but their belongings remain.
Let your goodness be all that remains.

When the image of the Beloved dances, 405
so does the soul.
So do countless stars in the sky and whole universes.
In the house of the heart,
no matter which tune is played,
that helpless body, too, starts dancing.

Fasting is the touchstone of good and bad. 406
Don't ask me how that could be.
This came from the One who is beyond questions.
Fasting is the divine food
which comes from beyond the sky.
It makes you and everything better.

407   Day brought me Your troubles and fights.
Night filled my head with Your Love.
But, all this is not the business of day or night.
This is my business.
How could those two lame donkeys carry my load?

408   The day when all beings annihilate themselves
and ascend to the height of Absence,
we shall see whose swords are stained with blood
and which beings have been so lucky
as to have had their blood shed.

On those days when the Beloved doesn't appear,   409
His image comes and stays in my eyes.
The most amazing thing is
that He is right in my heart,
yet my heart remains confused.

If you close your eyes to the pleasures of the Earth,   410
your heart will become your eye
and a different world will appear to you.
If you quit being full of your self,
you will be admired for everything you do.

411 Your artistry cut a piece of reed
     from the sugar cane field
     for lips which are sweet like sugar.
     That piece of reed drank so much wine
     from Your sweet lips
     that now it is always drunk and exalted.

412 Your hair, which has fallen over your sugar lips,
     intends to kill your slaves.
     Who would give such beauty in exchange for nothing?
     Who else would kick that lover
     when that lover is down?

After I was captured by the Beloved's Love,   413
my crying kept my neighbors from sleeping at night.
Now, my wailing has diminished,
but my Love has increased,
just as smoke is diminished when a flame grows.

Listen to the minstrel   414
to hear the secret of the lover's heart.
Keep turning around the heart
to the tune of his wailing.
What is that minstrel really saying?
"If you want to stay attached to Him,
tear the curtain and never diverge from His tune."

415   There are sparks coming
from the fires of the hearts of lovers.
They are the sighs of sorrow coming from the ones
who have given their hearts to the Beloved.
Haven't you heard that those sighs
go directly to the presence of God's compassion?

416   A little smile is enough to make us Your lover.
A short melody is enough to make
Your drunk exuberant.
Why do You draw the sword of sorrow to kill us
when a light lash of Your whip would be enough?

There is a Sultan who knows everything you hide.   417
Even if you boil quietly with anger, He knows it.
Everyone wants to speak eloquently.
But, I like the one who is the master of silence.

I am glad Your sorrow fits in my heart,   418
because it can rest in only bright places.
And, although that sorrow cannot fit
in either the Earth or the sky,
it is embedded in my heart
which is no bigger than the eye of a needle.

419   I couldn't get any pleasure from the present
      because of all of my troubles.
      I knew that nothing but the sorrow of the Beloved
      could cure me.
      I was thinking about telling Him this and that,
      but when we finally met,
      I couldn't even take one breath!

420   Night has gone, but where did it go?
      It has gone back to its origin.
      Just like everything else in existence,
      it has returned to its home.
      O night, when you are in that promised land,
      talk about us.
      Talk about each and all of our sufferings
      which have been delivered to us by Love.

Inside of my heart there is One with words so sweet   421
that it makes me forget
the story of Khosrow and Shirin.[32]
Sometimes He makes me angry and He is peaceful.
Sometimes the anger is His
and the peacefulness is mine.

I will go hundreds of miles beyond reason,   422
hundreds of miles beyond goodness and evil.
There are so many Beauties beyond this curtain,
and that includes my real being.
O ignorant one, I want to be in Love with Me!

---

[32] A love story about the Persian Shah Khosrow Parviz II (590-628 CE) and the Armenian Princess Shirin.

423 I pray, "May this moon-like Beauty
live a hundred years!"
Although my heart became the target
for His arrows of sorrow,
that was just my heart
dying in the dust of His threshold as it whispered,
"O how sweet is obedience to His will!"

424 Hundreds of oxen rumps
could not be thicker than your skin!
You are such a stone that even Moses's staff [33]
could not soften you!
O you frigid one, so many winters
got together to make up your body!
Nothing could warm you up
except extreme suffering and the fires of hell.

---

[33] Refers to the story of Moses striking a rock with his staff to get water. Quran 2:60.

From dawn throughout the morning,   425
the morning breeze is passing by,
scattering the fragrance of musk.
Smell that fragrance.
Think about where that breeze is coming from.
Why do you sleep? Wake up!
Life is passing by. Musk's caravan is passing by.
Be that sweet scent. Try.

This chosen one of God [34]   426
resembles a rose, always smiling.
He is not bitter.
Sugar does not have that quality.
He is the light of the lantern,
and his head is not iron, but clear glass.

---

[34] Quran 24:35.

427 A lover knows nothing but humiliation.
Where does he go at night except to Your quarters?
Don't get mad if he kisses Your hair.
What else could an insane one do
except bite his chains?

428 Courtesy and coquetry are not for lovers.
In the sect of Love, lovers are brave and generous.
Lovers are not coy.
It would be silly if Jacob acted like Joseph.

Know this very well: a lover cannot be a man 429
of any earthly religion.
In the religion of Love, there is no faith, no blasphemy.
There is no body, no soul, no heart, no reason.
Whoever has any of these is not a lover.

Once this Love arrived, all other loves disappeared. 430
Because of my longing for You,
I was burned and turned into ashes.
My ashes scattered and disappeared.
Then, they came back,
forming thousands of shapes again.

431   Your Love turns every place of worship into a tavern.
      Your Love sets a bazaar of idols aflame.
      Your sorrow's hands, like thieves,
      reach out everywhere and grab us in both worlds.

432   At the moment Your Love resolves to shed blood,
      my soul will fly out from this body's cage.
      If someone has the chance of kissing Your sugar lips,
      he becomes an infidel if he doesn't commit that sin.

If the Beloved would allow me to sit with Him 433
for just one moment,
my mind and heart would experience
so many different joys and pleasures.
Alas, I could build mills
in hundreds of different places,
but the lack of water delays my job.

Love has no beginning, no end. 434
Love is eternal.
So many people search for Love!
On the Day of Resurrection,
all will be denied entry into the Divine Temple
except lovers.

435 The nicest thing about Love
is that it is the source of troubles.
One is not a lover if he fears troubles.
One has to be brave in the business of Love.
When his soul catches the fire of Love,
a lover has to give up his soul.

436 Your Love took sanity away from this world.
Your separation became death.
It is still killing me.
I would not give away my heart
for a hundred thousand lives.
Yet, one of Your smiles took it away for free.

Sorrow which wouldn't dare come close   437
to the hearts of lovers
turns around cold-hearted, hopeless people.
There is such a giant sea inside of a lover's heart
that its waves make the sky turn.

Don't hide Your news from me.   438
You just don't want me to smile.
In fact, that message cannot be hidden.
Placing a sign which reads "Dungeon"
on the gate of the garden
doesn't make it one.

439 This lover's work is to recite poems.
In order to call for the Beauty
whose traces do not appear in this world,
one either tells stories about the bait and the trap,
or about giving up one's house and store.

440 A sage who was advancing on the way to Absence
passed through the sea of existence like wind.
But from his existence,
he still had a small piece of hair.
In the eyes of Absence, that hair appeared
like a rope belt
worn by someone who was not a true Muslim.

You have to do something deep inside of you.   441
One cannot untie this knot by listening to stories.
The fountain inside of the house
is better than a river outside.

On the way to Love,   442
each lover must either annihilate himself
or give up his life in death.
Some say,
"Love's goal is to drink water
from the Fountain of Life."
These are just empty words, O lover,
just empty words.

443 If fortune smiles on your face awhile,
don't take it too seriously.
After making you drunk,
fortune will move on, choosing others to embrace.

444 If thorns of sorrow were to cover both worlds,
a camel would not mind.
If troubles were to stain souls and whole universes,
a lover would still stay free and clear,
because Love is his cleaner.

If I continue to bear the pain of Your separation   445
a little bit longer,
my dress, my soul and everyone else's soul
will burn to ashes.
But, if I let out just one scream of pain,
my mouth will spit such a fire
that not only my mouth,
but both worlds will burn to ashes.

The one who knows that majestic King of kings   446
ascends without heart, without mind
to a perfect home.
The one who doesn't become crazy
after seeing Your face
is the one to call insane.

447   No one can ever take the ball away from Your mallet.
No matter how hard and sincerely they search,
without Your help,
no one can reach union with You.
If Joseph had had the same vision as Jacob,
he still would not have been able
to catch even the scent of Your beautiful dress.

448   You said, "The thing which comes
from the deceitful self
is like an arrow in the back from a traitor."
Yes, the bray of a donkey is bad,
but worse is the sound which comes from its behind.

The heart which takes in sorrow 449
will be filled indefinitely with divine joy.
That heart will be beyond the revolutions of the sky.
How can the seeds of sorrow be sown in any heart
when it is suspended in the sixth level of heaven?

The one who accepts sorrow rejoices with You 450
and, with Your light,
becomes the Sun of the Universe.
He becomes Your confidant.
If the mysteries of the Universe
are not hidden from You,
how could the secrets of the mind
be hidden from Your confidant?

451   What could a scorpion do to one
      who drinks Your sherbet?
      How could poison affect me
      when I have reached Your sugar lips?
      You are the alchemy of Nothingness.
      How lucky is the man who is maturing in Your fire!

452   Those ruby lips know how to sell sugar,
      how to drink the wine of Absence.
      If I had permission,
      I would say whose lips they really are.
      But, I am a slave to the One
      who knows how to keep silence.

When His lips become obstinate and belligerent, 453
sugar and honey are scattered over both worlds.
Hear this from me:
if you see a moon in your weary heart,
it is Shams of Tabriz.

I am sad because of that moon-faced Beloved 454
who can tie a glorious belt around the Moon.
He is not satisfied with my love and joy,
and He keeps secretly smiling so sweetly
when He sees me crying.

455   The sources of all troubles
      are the greed and the ambition of the self.
      Those who crave food and women
      are always in trouble.
      A bird which has fallen into a trap because of the bait
      remains in a cage all its life,
      just hanging from the ceiling.

456   You called your Beloved a moon.
      But, what is the Moon?
      You called him a sultan. But, who is the Sultan?
      You asked me why I get up when it is still night.
      If I am always with the Sun, what is night?

The bird which is raised in the garden of the master   457
becomes obstinate and,
at the same time, drunk and coy.
But, if it wants to guide the master,
it will be caught,
because the pride of early flight will have deceived it.

The bird from the country of cowards   458
flies feebly and only on this side.
There is a bird with the talent to be a sultan,
a bird which comes out of an egg of the phoenix.
That bird flies only in the direction
of the land with no direction,
that crazy wild country, the mountain of Qaf.[35]

---

[35] A legendary mountain surrounding the Earth. Where the Simurgh lives.

459   Being and non-being are troublesome

for the one who knows

the true nature of existence and Non-existence.

The one who is free from creation

and turns into Creator

is not bothered by attributes and actions.

460   A beloved who stays in the house

taking care of it is no good.

Even if that one shows affection for you,

he is not loyal.

The true Beloved is the one who,

in your final hour

opens thousands of doors

and shows you the garden of heaven.

The beloved who pays no attention to us,   461
who stays at home all the time playing the ney,
who stays behind the curtain,
that beloved is no use to us.
The true Beloved comes to the Tavern,
singing and playing music until midnight.

When the Beloved shines like the Sun,   462
lovers start dancing like particles.
The breeze of Love's spring brings everything to life.
The only branches not dancing are the dead ones.

463   I am lightning in this world.
The remains of your self are not a measure of Me.
Don't compare yourself with Me.
That is like poison, like victory over My player.
But, where is that player?
If you stay close to Me,
you will not find such games necessary.

464   I am a slave of the mind which has become crazy
because of that Beloved.
The heart which bleeds for Him
is worth hundreds of souls.
I swear by God,
even the Water of Life becomes jealous
of the tears flowing from the eyes of lovers.

His face resembles the bright side of the Moon. 465
His temperament is like that of the angels.
No, no! What are these comparisons?
What is the Moon? What are angels?
My soul, which is His slave, testifies,
"He resembles only Him."

Don't let worry 466
charm and control you like a snake.
When that peerless Moon decides to shine over you,
even the sky will be envious.

Rumi's *Dîvân-i Kebîr* is like a divine table for nourishing the heart and soul of humanity. This table has been open to everyone for almost 800 years now. In order to benefit from it, one has only to come to the table.

-Nevit O. Ergin

Appendices

Haqq

Haqq is the Arabic word for Truth. In Islamic contexts, it is also interpreted as right and reality. Al-Haqq [the Truth], is one of the names of God in the Qur'an. According to Wikipedia, it is often used to refer to God as the Ultimate Reality in Islam.

We have included the word Haqq at the bottom of each page of quatrains in this first volume of *The Rubáiyát of Rumi, The Ergin Translations* to honor Rumi and his tradition.

Notes on These Translations

Since the first English translation of forty-eight poems from Rumi's *Dîvân-i Kebîr* was published by R.A. Nicholson in 1898, Rumi has slowly, but surely become more and more well-known to the Western world. In particular, the first 23 years of our 21st century have seen an explosion of commentaries, research projects, and collections of Rumi's poetry. Rumi is shared through books, in sermons at places of worship, at colleges and universities and through social media.

So why these translations by Ergin? Just as there could never be too many new performances of Beethoven, there can never be too many collections of Rumi. Each brings a slightly different perspective to the world, and each perspective speaks in a voice which reaches the ones who need to hear it. And Rumi needs to be heard by everyone in this world, especially in times as tumultuous as these. He is recognized by many as the greatest and most prolific mystic poet of all time. We regard his poetry as sacred texts.

Nevit Ergin, Translator

Nevit Ergin (1928-2015) had been introduced to Rumi in 1956 by Hasan Lutfi Shushud (1902-1988), author of *Masters of Wisdom of Central Asia* and *Fakir Sözleri* and a Master of the Itlak Yolu Sufi Path of Annihilation and Absolute Liberation.

Ergin was looking for something which went beyond the lectures, books, philosophy courses, religion and everything else he had tried up to that point in his life. On one auspicious Sunday, he had occasion to meet Mr. Shushud. That day was the beginning of a lifelong friendship.

On one of his first visits, Ergin took with him a book of selected Rumi poems entitled *Gül Deste* [*Bouquet of Roses*] just published by the Turkish scholar, Abdülbakî Gölpinarli (1900-1982). When Ergin asked Mr. Shushud about the value of the book, Mr. Shushud went out into his garden, cut a long-stemmed rose, returned and gave it to him. Ergin pressed the rose between the pages of that book which he would carry with him for the rest of his life. Mr. Shushud proceeded to tell him that he would need to experience lots of hunger, lots of a type of breath work, and lots of mental suffering. Reading, discussing and fellowship would come later. He added, "If you choose one book, the *Dîvân-i Kebîr of Mevlânâ Celâleddîn Rumi* will do it."

It was not until the late 1980's that Ergin began "to know Mevlânâ." Although he was living in the United States, he continued to travel several times a year to Turkey. He first translated into English selections of Gölpinarli's Turkish translations of the *Dîvân-i Kebîr*, specifically, selections of the *Rubáiyát*. These were published by Hohm Press under the title, *Crazy as We Are*. The following year, 1993, Larson Publications published *Magnificent One*, a selection of ghazals [longer lyric poems, or odes] from the *Dîvân*. Ergin was encouraged by that publisher to translate what he thought was the entirety of the ghazals from Gölpinarli's Turkish translations. He accomplished the translations of those ghazals between 1992 and 2003, and they were published as the *Dîvân-i Kebîr of Mevlânâ Celâleddîn Rumi* (in 22 volumes) through his own publishing company, Echo Publications, and the Ministry of Culture of the Republic of Turkey. It was also in 1992 that he formed the non-profit organization, the Society for Understanding Mevlânâ.

Our Friendship

Hasan Shushud was also the one who introduced me to Rumi. When I stayed with him for a few weeks in 1972,[1] we visited a small building where he pointed out some large, ornate double doors, and said, "These are the doors to the house of Mevlânâ. One day you must get to know him."

The day before I left Istanbul, Nevit Ergin visited Mr. Shushud, Mr. Shushud introduced us, and that was for me the beginning. I went to work for Ergin in Michigan in his

---

[1]There is a more detailed account of my time with Mr. Shushud in Ergin's *The Sufi Path of Annihilation*, published by Inner Traditions in 2014.

nursery school, and although I stayed as his employee for only three years, we stayed friends until his death in 2015.

When he began translating Rumi, I helped him connect with publishers for his first two collections. With the first volume of the *Dîvân-i Kebîr* project in 1993, I was responsible for book design, printing and typesetting. I was also put on the board of the newly formed Society for Understanding Mevlânâ as a consultant, but my role was limited to working on the books.

Ergin was a plastic surgeon. Over the years, I visited him fairly frequently in his office. After the late 1980s, whenever he was between patients, he would invariably be translating a ghazal. He would read whatever he was translating to me, always excited, and me always nodding my head in agreement, but not understanding his excitement. It took another ten years for me to see why he so often said to me, "The *Dîvân* is like a mine field. You never know when it will blow your heart and mind."

Ergin moved back to live in Turkey from 1996 through 1999, and we did not reconnect on a regular basis until after I retired in 2012. During the interim, he published *Tales of a Modern Sufi*, as well as, with Will Johnson, *Insane with Love* and *Forbidden Rumi*. But, from 2012 until 2015, I spent one week a month helping him get his final works completed. During those three years, he completed a number of new short stories (as yet unpublished), *The Sufi Path of Annihilation*, a retranslation of *Volume 9* of the *Dîvân-i Kebîr*, *Unknown Rumi*, and *Mevlânâ Rubâîler* with Merâle Ekmekçioğlu. (See below)

The *Replica*

Over the years of traveling between the United States and Turkey, Ergin became good friends with Erdoğan Erol, the Director of the Mevlânâ Museum in Konya, Turkey. Thanks to Erol's support, the museum gave him permission to photograph some of the artwork of the *Dîvân-i Kebîr* housed in the museum (numbers 68 and 69), and in 1993, replications of those photos were printed in the first volume of Ergin's translations of the *Dîvân's* ghazals.

Then, in 2006, the Turkish Ministry of Culture and the Mevlânâ Museum gave Ergin permission to commission the production of a microfiche of the entire hand-written, two-volume set of that *Dîvân*; to take color photographs of all of its artwork; and, most important, to reproduce one thousand copies of the set. We refer to this set as the *Replica*. Thanks to the financial backing of Edmond Gorginian, the publication was made a reality in 2007 through Echo Publications and the Society for Understanding Mevlânâ.

Ergin's desire was to make it possible for more people to read the *Dîvân* in its original, hand-written Farsi and for more people to be able to translate from the original Farsi directly into English. He set out to get the *Replica* placed in libraries and universities across the United States and Europe and to make it available to purchase on the internet.

And, of course, once Ergin had the *Replica* in his hands, thanks to the help of those who could read the original text, he was able to confirm his own translations.

Ergin's *Mevlânâ Rubâîler*

Ergin was profoundly aware of the criticism that his English translations were from the Turkish and not directly from the original Farsi. As a result, as he translated the *Rubáiyát* from Gölpinarli's Turkish, he consulted with scholars from Stanford University who were able to read the *Replica* text. But, he also was determined to publish a book with a photograph of each rubai in its hand-written original Farsi, accompanied by a Turkish translation, and an English translation as well. He believed this would encourage others to explore each of Rumi's quatrains on their own.

Ergin worked on the English translations himself from 2007 until just before his passing in 2015, and during that same period, worked on the Turkish translations with Merâl

Ekmekçioğlu, who had *Mevlânâ Rubâîler* published in 2016 through Sarayönü Gazete–Matbaa in Konya, Turkey.

The Rubáiyát of Rumi, The Ergin Translations

Unlike *Mevlânâ Rubâîler*, our four-volume set is an English-only version. Our goal was to provide a more affordable version, and one which could be easily picked up to read in any place, at any time.

We chose to publish Ergin's translations of the *Rubáiyát of Rumi* for several reasons. Although selections of his translations have been published before, this is the first time his translations of all 1,867 quatrains will have been published - in English only - in their entirety. But we also chose to publish these quatrains because they are short, yet remarkably powerful. In some of them, an idea can hit you square in the eye and rattle your whole perception of life. Some may speak to you superficially and others at the deepest of levels.

In finalizing the translations for publication, I was able to collaborate with my dear friend, Shahzad Mazhar, who has studied Middle Eastern poetry, who is able to read the original medieval Farsi texts of the *Dîvân-i Kebîr Replica*, and who loves Rumi's poetry.

Clearly, Ergin's work is not a word-by-word translation, and he made no effort to adhere to the quatrain format. However, the remarkable spiritual work which he accomplished in his lifetime allowed him to capture more deeply the essence of Rumi's poetry. That said, since English was Ergin's second language (after Turkish), others have questioned the authenticity of some of his word choices. Thanks to Shahzad, I was able to confirm that every one of Ergin's translated quatrains was matched in its essence to the *Replica* text.

Of note is that the more earthly quatrains needed more of our attention to the English than those reflecting the concepts of Absence or reflecting Absence itself.

Also of note is the translation of Rubai 809 in Volume 2. In a bow to Hasan Shushud, Ergin added footnotes to show the concordance of the language used in Shushud's *Masters of Wisdom of Central Asia*:

> All forms and shapes are from base matter.*
> The Divine† is the One who forms them.
> The world of Essence‡
> doesn't come to the world of appearances,**
> but it manifests in the world of appearances.

*Hasan Shushud, *Masters of Wisdom of Central Asia* (Rochester, VT: Inner Traditions, 2014), 167. Heyâlâ [matter].
†Shushud, *Masters*, 172. Lâhût [divinity].
‡Shushud, *Masters*, 158. Ayn [essence].
**Shushud, *Masters*, 172. Nâsût [humanity].

And finally of note, in books and articles and online, the spellings of names differ wildly according to language and religious tradition. For example, for the Rumi biographer Ahmet Eflâkî, his first name is seen as Ahmet, Ahmed and Ahmad, and Eflâkî is seen as Eflaki and Aflaki. If any verbiage is quoted in our four volumes, the source spellings were used with no effort made to reach consistency or "correct" English spelling.

Rumi recited his verses in couplets. The rubai is the shortest form he used, each rubai being two couplets, or a quatrain. In fact, rubai is the Arabic word for quatrain. Each rubai expresses a complete, epigrammatic idea. The first, second and fourth lines rhyme, while the third line is usually free.

This form has been known in classic Islamic literature since the 10th century. However, it was an unknown form in the Western world until the late 1850's when the English poet Edward Fitzgerald (1809-1883) published his translation of the *Rubaiyat of Omar Khayyam* (1048-1131).

The first *Rubaiyat of Rumi*, selections translated into English by A.J. Arberry (1905-1973) appeared in 1949 under the title, *Mystical Poems of Rumi 1, First Selection, Poems 1-200.*[2]

Our current publication of *The Rubáiyát of Rumi, The Ergin Translations*, includes all of Rumi's quatrains found in the Osman al-Mavlavi compilation, described below.

There are 1,867 quatrains total in our four volumes, although 52 of the quatrains are duplicates. Considering the immense amount of material that had to be hand-copied for the *Dîvân*, it is no wonder there are so many duplicates. We have included each one as it appears in the *Replica*, making a note in our concordance where each set of duplicates can be found.

The Works of Rumi

Rumi created numerous works, all with the same messaging, but delivered in different forms. They include the *Dîvân-i Kebîr* (two volumes of poetry in various meters and forms including the ghazal, terci-bend, murabbe and rubai), the *Mesnevî* (six volumes of poetry all in one meter), *Mektubat* (letters), *Mecâlis-i Seb'a* (seven sermons) and *Fîhi Mâ Fîhi* (conversations).

For many years, Rumi's work most well-known to the West was the *Mesnevî*, a collection of stories and anecdotes written in AA, BB, CC couplets. He dictated this great work to his last close companion, Çelebi Hüsameddin (1225-1284), beginning in 1258 and continuing until his death in 1273. It is the most interpreted work in the Islamic world after the Quran and the Hadith.[3]

His second most well-known work is his *Dîvân-i Kebîr* (also known as *Dîvân-i Shems-i Tebriz*). *Dîvân-i Kebîr* means "big notebook," dîvân being the name given to the notebook in which writers collect their poems. Rumi's reputation among so many audiences as the greatest mystic love poet of all time is thanks in part to the work found in his *Dîvân*.

---

[2] Nevit O. Ergin, *Private Notes*.
[3] Erdoğan Erol, *Mevlânâ's Life, Works and the Mevlânâ Museum* (Konya: Altunari Ofset Ltd. Şti, 2005),27-36.

The Origins of the *Dîvân-i Kebîr*

As mentioned before, after he met the Sufi mystic, Shams of Tabriz, Rumi began reciting poems for his *Dîvân*. We do not know of any one poem which Rumi actually wrote down. He recited his poems extemporaneously, responding to various questions and events or reflecting on his own mystical experiences. His words were written down by scribes known as Kâtib-i Esrar (Secretaries of Secrets).

Unfortunately, Rumi's *Dîvân* was not compiled during his lifetime. However, in the next century, a number of compilations of the notes of these scribes were created.

The Hasan ibni Osman-al Mavlavi Compilation

We used only the one compilation which Ergin had photographed and eventually published as the *Replica*. It is a two-volume compilation, currently housed in the Mevlânâ Museum in Konya, Turkey as numbers 68 and 69. It was compiled by Hasan ibni Osman-al Mavlavi between July 2, 1367 and October 13, 1368. It is in two large volumes, measuring 17 inches tall and 12½ inches wide, containing a total of 326 pages. The work is in Farsi, the language of poetry of Rumi's time, with some words scattered throughout in Arabic, Turkish, and even Greek. The total number of individual verses exceeds 44,000, and they are formed into rubáiyát, ghazals, terci-bends and murabbes.

As we have previously mentioned, there are 1,867 rubáiyát, or quatrains, in the Osman-al Mavlavi compilation.

The compilation has 3,327 ghazals. The ghazal is a longer form of lyric love poetry dating back to 7th century Arabic poetry. Its theme is often that of the pain of separation. Each verse is a couplet of the same poetic meter, with a rhyme scheme of AA, BA, CA, DA and so on. The couplets of each ghazal fit under the umbrella of one theme, but each couplet is independent in meaning, and the connection to the other couplets is sometimes obscure. The final couplet includes the author's pen name. In Rumi's *Dîvân*, Rumi often ends with the mention of Shams of Tabriz, thereby attributing authorship to him.

The compilation has 37 terci-bends. The terci-bend form is a didactic poem. It has the same stylistic features of the ghazal, but each couplet is followed by a couplet with its own separate rhyme scheme. The terci-bend is a much longer form, and the couplets are divided into stanzas of five to ten couplets each. One couplet is repeated at the end of each stanza and each stanza "bends back" to express the theme of the first section in a different way.

The compilation has six murabbes. The murabbe form developed out of the quatrain form. It is actually a series of quatrains, each one tied thematically. Each verse features the same final line.

This compilation was first translated from Farsi into Turkish by the Turkish scholar Abdülbakî Gölpinarli. He published the first volume of his seven volume *Dîvân-i Kebîr Mevlânâ Celâleddîn* in 1957 and the final one in 1974.

For his *Dîvân-i Kebîr Mevlânâ Celâleddîn*, Gölpinarli also referenced three other sources: (1) the *Dîvân* registered at the Library of the University of Istanbul, No. 334, which was compiled in the 15th century; (2) the *Dîvân* owned by Gölpinarli himself, prepared in 1691 in Baghdad; and (3) the eight volumes of the *Kulliyât-e shams yâdîwân-é kebîr -e mawlânâ jalâluddîn* prepared by Persian scholar Badî'uzzamân Forûzânfar (1904-1979) which were completed in 1965. However, Gölpinarli considered the Osman-al Mavlavi compilation his most reliable source.[4]

Other Contributors
to the West's Knowledge of Rumi

In the 1950's, Gölpinarli and Forûzânfar were the two scholars most responsible for increasing the Western world's interest and knowledge of Rumi. Ergin knew both of them.

---
[4] Mevlânâ Celâleddîn Rumi Nevit O. Ergin, Translator, Divan-i Kebir, Meter 1 (Walla Walla, WA: Turkish Republic Ministry of Culture & Current, 1995), vii; Ergin, Private Notes, 2015.

Gölpinarli was from a family with a Mevlevi tradition. His Farsi and Arabic were strong and his life was devoted to the study of Rumi. He translated into Turkish not only the *Dîvân-i Kebîr*, but all of the rest of Rumi's works as well. The last part of his life was spent at the Mevlânâ Museum in Konya cataloging all of their works related to Rumi.

Forûzânfar was a renowned modern scholar of Persian literature, which consists mostly of poetry, and is considered the Persian authority on Rumi. He produced considerable critical works and commentaries on Rumi in Persian which made it easier for Western scholars to translate Rumi. Most importantly, he researched various compilations to determine the full scope of Rumi's poetry and included all of Rumi's ghazals, terci-bends, and rubáiyát in a single work of eight volumes entitled, the *Kulliyât-e shams*, mentioned above. As part of his research, he determined which verses were Rumi's and which were created by others, but mistakenly attributed to Rumi.

We would be remiss not to mention some of the other scholars who gave the West its introductions to Rumi, contributing a foundation for further study. These include but are not limited to E.H. Whinfield (1836-1922), Reynold A. Nicholson (1868-1945), A.J. Arberry (1905-1973), Annemarie Schimmel (1922-2003), and the Turkish scholar Şefik Can (1909-2005). The American poet and professor Coleman Barks (1937-) has provided Americanized versions of Rumi. Barks is perhaps the most responsible for making Rumi the most popular poet in North America today.

And, as we mentioned at the opening of these notes, in the first 23 years of our 21st century, there has been an explosion of commentaries, research projects, and collections of Rumi's poetry by contributors too numerous to name. Such an explosion may be saying that if we haven't taken Rumi very seriously before, now is the time to do so.

And, we look forward to the future as others continue to contribute to our knowledge of this greatest of mystic poets.

The Importance of Islam in Rumi's Life

Rumi was raised a Muslim in Balkh, (present-day Afghanistan), his family eventually settling in Konya, Turkey, in 1228 at the request of the Seljuk ruler Keyqubâd I. At that time, Rumi was 21 years old. His father, Muhammed Bahaeddin Veled, was the Sultânü'l Ûlemâ [Sultan of the Scholars], and once in Konya, he assumed responsibilities of heading a medresse [theological school] there. When his father passed in 1231, Rumi became his successor, taking on all of his father's duties, students and disciples.

By then, Rumi was already a scholar of many disciplines, an expert on Sharia [Islamic religious law], the Quran, and the Hadith [sayings and traditions of the Prophet Muhammad].[5] Even after he met Shams of Tabriz, he stated:

> As long as my soul stays in my body,
>
> I am a slave of the Quran
>
> and the dust on the path of Muhammad.
>
> If anyone interprets my words
>
> differently than this,
>
> I will break with him and reject his words.
>
> -Rubai 735 (Volume 2)

Naturally, we would expect Rumi's poetry to reflect his Islamic Tradition. However, Rumi's message is universal. His Islamic roots do not change his appeal for those of all religious backgrounds, nor does it diminish the existence of other messengers of God from other religious traditions and the truth of their messages. As he clearly states:

> I came here to unify,
>
> not to divide.[6]

---

[5]Erol, *Mevlânâ's Life*, 12-13.
[6]Erol, *Mevlânâ's Life*, 7.

As he also clearly states:

> There is neither question nor answer
> on the way to Love,
> but only a mystery.
> The lover never answers to any human orders.
> This is a matter of Absence, not existence.
>
> -Rubai 1314 (Volume 3)

Islamic and Sufi Terms Commonly Used in Rumi's Poetry

Eid [Arabic] A religious holiday celebrating the end of Ramadan.

Kaaba [Arabic "the cube"] An ancient stone structure built as a house of monotheistic worship. Located inside the Grand Mosque (the most sacred Al-Masjid al Harām) in Mecca. Considered to be the center of the Muslim world and a unifying focal point for Islamic worship.

Qibla [Arabic] The direction Muslims face to pray, fixed as the direction of the Kaaba.

Ramadan [Arabic] The ninth month of the Islamic calendar, observed by Muslims worldwide as a month of fasting, prayer, reflection and community.

Sema [Turkish] A Sufi ceremony performed as a remembrance of God. In the Mevlevi Order, which was established after the death of Mevlânâ Celâleddîn Rumi by his son, Sultan Veled, the performers are known as Whirling Dervishes.

The Role of Music in Rumi's Life

Rumi introduced "turning" accompanied by music to his disciples in a ceremony known as Sema. During the ceremony, participants allowed the music and their turning to carry them into an ecstatic state. Because of the practice, after Rumi's passing and with the formal organization of the Mevlevi Order of Sufism by Rumi's son, Sultan Veled, members of the order were and still are known as the Whirling Dervishes.

Although Islam had strict prohibitions against such type of ceremonies, there was great support of the arts under the Seljuk rule in Konya and a pronounced freedom which made it possible for the Sema ceremony to take place.

According to Turkish scholar Abdülbakî Gölpinarli, "Mevlânâ would easily be impressed by daily events and would start reciting his feelings while he was performing semâ in ecstasy and pour them into the mould [sic] of measure and rhyme."[7] Is it any wonder, then, that Rumi would make so many references to musical instruments in his poetry?

---

[7] Erol, *Mevlânâ's Life*, 32.

Poet-Musician Playing a Tanbur
Excavated ceramic from Anatolia, early 13th century.

Image Credit: bpkBildagentur/Museum of Islamic Art/ Georg Niedermeiswer/ Art Resource, NY.

Musical Instruments Commonly Referred to in Rumi's Poetry

Ney (or nay, from Persian nāy meaning reed, pipe.) The end-blown flute of the Middle East, from North Africa to Iran and the Caucasus. Made of cane (or sometimes wood or metal), it is often the only wind instrument regularly used in classical ensembles of Middle-Eastern music. Its characteristically breathy tone gives much scope for 'programme' effects, like the blowing of the wind or the shepherd's mourning. Famously, Rumi begins his *Mesnevî* with the couplet:

> "Listen to this Ney, while it's complaining,
> The story of separation from God it's explaining."[8]

Rebab (or rabab.) The oldest known Arabic word for a bowed instrument today denoting a large number of instruments played from North Africa across Asia to Indonesia. Pear- and boat-shaped rabābs hollowed in one piece, held downwards, and consisting of a membrane belly and two or three thick gut strings were particularly common. Flat, round, trapezoidal and rectangular bodies are also found. The single-stringed "poet's fiddle" of the Arab Middle East has a small round or cylindrical body that appears skewered by a narrow neck, and is played especially in self-accompaniment to narrations.

---

[8]Erol, *Mevlânâ's Life*, 31.

Tanbur A very early name for a long lute with a full metallic timbre, today denoting many varieties over the Middle East from Syria and Iraq to Turkestan in Central Asia. It has a small pear-shaped body, a long neck, many gut frets and two or three double metal strings. It has faithfully preserved the outer appearance of the ancient lutes of Babylonia and Egypt.

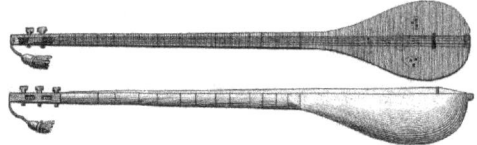

Saz The 'long lute of Turkey' played also to the east up to Azerbaijan on the Caspian and in Europe in local varieties across to Albania on the Adriatic and Greece. Similar to the tanbur, it has a long thin neck, three double metal strings, and a pear-shaped body that has, from the side, a characteristic appearance of a deep scoop, deepest at the level of the bridge.

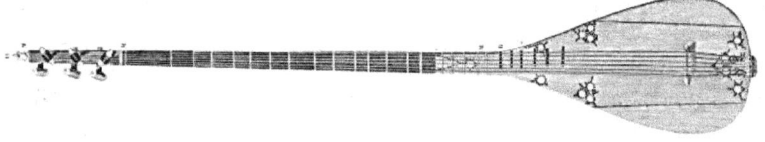

Tambourine A frame drum consisting of a single skin and pairs of metallic jingles placed within the frame. Essential to much classical music, it appears in the Middle Ages first in the Middle East and by 1300 C.E. in Europe. Over the Middle East and North Africa, tambourines are played with subtle use of both hands in the membrane, the fingers of the holding hand participating, whereas common European manner involves striking and shaking.

Zurna (or surna, surnāy, from Persian sūr meaning feast, and nāy meaning reed, pipe.) The Eastern representative of the shawm family, an end-blown oboe played to Central Eurasia, western Asia and North Africa. It consists of seven finger holes, one thumb hole, and several 'vent' holes. Historically played outdoors during festive events and to gather crowds in order to make official announcements, it produces a constantly loud, high-pitched and piercing sound.

The Story of Joseph and Jacob

Rumi mentions Joseph and Jacob in his rubáiyát more often than characters from any other story. Not only is the story of Joseph and his father Jacob given prominence in the Quran, but it is a dominant reference throughout Persian, Urdu and Arabic poetry as well, where Joseph is the symbol of the one who has left or been pulled away and Jacob is the symbol of the yearning lover.

The story of Joseph is shared in both the Bible (Genesis chapters 37, 38-50) and the Quran (which names its twelfth chapter, "Joseph"). There are slight differences in the two accounts. This summary is based on the story as it is presented in the Quran.

In his lifetime, Joseph went through intense suffering, but he was also given many spiritual blessings.

Of the family's twelve boys, Joseph was his father Jacob's favorite. Because of their jealousy, the brothers took Joseph into the wilderness and threw him into a well. They returned home, lying to their father, saying that his favorite son had been eaten by a wolf.

In the meantime, some strangers found Joseph, pulled him out of the well, and sold him as a slave to a prosperous Egyptian man and his family.

After some years of working for the Egyptians, Joseph was falsely accused of committing adultery with the Egyptian's wife. He was unjustly thrown into jail at the same time as two other men. Joseph successfully interpreted the dreams of these two other men. Eventually, one of the two was released and returned to his job of serving the King.

Several years passed. The King had two confusing dreams which no one could interpret. The former inmate remembered Joseph's talent, so he returned to the jail to ask Joseph for his help. Joseph saw the dreams as a prophecy for the entire region: there would be seven years of plenty, followed by seven years of famine. The inmate shared this interpretation with the King. The King was so pleased with the interpretation's clarity and vision that he summoned Joseph from jail and put him in charge of Egypt's granaries.

Joseph prepared Egypt for the famine by storing grain during the seven years of plenty. During the years of famine, Joseph's brothers, sent by their father, came to Egypt to purchase grain. They didn't recognize Joseph, although he recognized them. He sent them back home with grain, as well as his shirt.

Jacob had become blind with grief after the disappearance of his favorite son. As soon as his other sons arrived back home from Egypt, he caught the scent of Joseph's shirt. In this way, he came to know that Joseph was still alive. Then, when the sons covered his face with the shirt, Jacob regained his eyesight.

Finally, at Joseph's invitation, the entire tribe joined Joseph in Egypt to live happy and prosperous lives.

Both Joseph and Jacob are considered prophets.

The Concordance

With this publication, as Ergin intended with *Mevlânâ Rubâîler*, we are not trying to create controversy. Like so many others, we believe that these are sacred texts. And, we believe the more clear water poured into the river, the better. We encourage all who are interested to compare *The Ergin Translations* with the work of other translators.

You will notice in this Concordance that we have included a source for Ergin's original translations of Ergin's *Mevlânâ Rubâîler*, as well as for those of Turkish scholar Abdülbakî Gölpinarli, Persian scholar Badî'uzzamân Forûzânfar and Turkish scholar and spiritual leader Şefik Can. We have depended on Ergin's source numbers for these three. As Ergin states in the Translator's Note to his *Mevlânâ Rubâîler*, "For each of the quatrains, there are three sources cited. This is due to conflicting scholarship as regards original material."[9]

Also included in our Concordance are the rubai numbers corresponding to the work, *The Quatrains of Rumi*, by the Persian scholars Ibrahim Gamard and Rawan Farhadi. The Gamard-Farhadi book is well-researched, and we were able to ascertain from it any of the few Forûzânfar concordances which were missing from Ergin's work.

---

[9]Nevit Ergin & Merâle Ekmekçioğlu, *Mevlânâ Rubâîler* (Konya: Saray Medya Yayinlari, 2016), 13.

Rubáiyát	Duplicate numbers	Ergin	Gölpinarli	Forûzânfar	Şefik Can	Farhadi Gamard
\multicolumn{7}{c}{**VOLUME 1**}					
\multicolumn{7}{c}{*Dîvân-i Kebîr Replica, Volume 2, Page 129b*}					
1		28-1	15-1	60	60	632
2		28-2	15-2	50	50	1246
3		29-2	15-3	7	7	1363
4		30-1	15-4	65	65	551
5	1155	29-3	15-4	30	30	1511
6		29-4	15-4	55	55	1913
7		31-3	16-7	20	20	894
8		31-4	16-8	9	9	1476
9		34-3	16-9	67	67	553
10		34-4	16-10	42	42	589
11	1162	35-3	16-11	47	47	1250
12		32-3	16-12	12	12	951
13		33-4	16-13	61	61	312
14		33-3	16-14	41	41	75
\multicolumn{7}{c}{*Dîvân-i Kebîr Replica, Volume 2, Page 130a*}					
15		33-1	17-15	59	59	922
16		36-2	17-16	17	17	685
17		36-1	17-17	46	46	1851
18		36-4	17-18	58	58	517
19		37-3	17-19	44	44	716
20		38-2	17-20	48	48	100
21		38-1	17-21	23	23	1478
22		38-3	17-22	3	3	1937
23		39-3	18-23	21	21	897
24		39-4	18-24	43	43	1187
25		40-2	18-25	25	25	1629
26		41-1	18-26	26	26	1429
27		41-2	18-27	5	5	1260
28		41-3	18-28	49	49	1470
29		40-4	18-29	40	40	1592
30		41-4	18-30	13	13	545

Rubáiyát	Duplicate numbers	Ergin	Gölpinarli	Forûzânfar	Şefik Can	Farhadi Gamard
31		42-3	18-31	6	6	1809
32		43-3	19-32	53	53	1157
33		42-4	19-33	51	51	920
34		43-1	19-34	38	38	35
35		44-2	19-35	70	70	1147
36		44-3	19-36	37	37	216
37		45-1	19-37	69	69	983
38		45-3	19-38	2	2	531
39		44-1	19-39	24	24	39
40		45-4	---	15	15	1338
41		46-1	20-40	39	39	618
42		46-4	24-1	81	94	1263
43		47-1	24-2	95	108	377
44		47-3	24-3	79	92	744
45		48-3	24-4	102	115	1308
46	1185	48-4	24-5	97	110	375
47		49-3	24-6	98	111	374

Dîvân-i Kebîr Replica, Volume 2, Page 130b

48		49-4	24-7	99	112	378
49		47-4	24-8	91	104	945
50		50-1	25-9	92	105	1124
51		50-2	25-10	83	96	746
52		50-4	25-11	82	95	1957
53		51-1	25-12	87	100	1301
54		51-2	25-13	75	88	740
55		52-2	25-14	85	98	382
56		53-3	25-15	101	114	1887
57		53-1	25-16	88	101	1303
58		53-4	26-17	93	106	1437
59		54-4	28-1	125	143	157
60		64-3	28-2	184	202	1497
61		65-1	28-3	395	413	1314
62		63-2	28-4	114	132	58

Rubáiyát	Duplicate numbers	Ergin	Gölpinarli	Forûzânfar	Şefik Can	Farhadi Gamard
63		63-4	28-5	277	295	1518
64		66-1	28-6	429	447	568
65		55-1	28-7	386	404	1329
66		65-4	28-8	120	138	1198
67		67-1	29-9	129	147	300
68		67-4	29-10	168	186	1387
69		55-2	29-11	399	417	40
70		69-1	29-12	206	224	74
71		68-4	29-13	321	339	1950
72		59-1	29-14	182	200	586
73		55-4	29-15	158	176	1911
74		56-1	29-16	255	336	733
75		58-1	29-17	212	230	305
76		57-4	30-18	127	145	440
77		59-3	30-19	107	125	7
78		57-3	30-20	254	272	764
79		60-4	30-21	119	137	622
80		56-4	30-22	236	254	698

Dîvân-i Kebîr Replica, Volume 2, Page 131a

Rubáiyát	Duplicate numbers	Ergin	Gölpinarli	Forûzânfar	Şefik Can	Farhadi Gamard
81		60-2	30-23	220	238	336
82		62-1	30-24	198	216	581
83		78-4	30-25	229	247	1350
84		79-4	31-26	126	144	1818
85		77-1	31-27	149	167	1242
86		78-3	31-28	345	363	1168
87		77-3	31-29	318	336	676
88		77-2	31-30	381	399	223
89		78-1	31-31	370	388	1471
90		71-1	31-32	322	340	1826
91		70-2	31-33	389	407	230
92		75-2	32-34	217	235	533
93		76-2	32-35	216	234	1620
94		71-2	32-36	172	190	914

Rubáiyát	Duplicate numbers	Ergin	Gölpinarli	Forûzânfar	Şefik Can	Farhadi Gamard
95		73-1	32-37	311	329	1182
96		70-4	32-38	309	327	228
97		72-2	32-39	403	421	960
98		72-3	32-40	362	380	1746
99	1229	58-2	32-41	274	292	973
100		63-3	33-42	385	403	1759
101		72-1	33-43	388	406	944
102		76-1	33-44	109	127	45
103		69-4	33-45	117	135	202
104		75-1	33-46	235	253	1719
105		87-2	33-47	267	285	34
106		83-3	33-48	423	441	1615
107		80-4	33-49	243	261	38
108		80-2	33-50	405	423	42
109		83-2	34-51	361	379	1883
110		86-1	34-52	137	155	928
111		82-1	34-53	335	353	1795
112		84-3	34-54	153	171	1845
113		85-2	34-56	328	346	1931

Dîvân-i Kebîr Replica, Volume 2, Page 131b

Rubáiyát	Duplicate numbers	Ergin	Gölpinarli	Forûzânfar	Şefik Can	Farhadi Gamard
114		85-1	34-56	341	359	1932
115		84-2	34-57	104	122	1718
116		85-3	34-58	319	337	1958
117	1295	89-4	35-59	169	187	615
118		88-3	35-60	351	369	725
119	1276	89-3	35-61	250	268	1785
120		88-2	35-62	278	296	924
121		87-4	35-63	205	223	677
122		88-1	35-64	360	378	1895
123		92-1	35-65	148	166	1427
124		90-4	35-66	176	194	1559
125		91-2	35-67	186	204	456
126		91-1	36-68	131	149	1298

Rubáiyát	Duplicate numbers	Ergin	Gölpinarli	Forûzânfar	Şefik Can	Farhadi Gamard
127		91-4	36-69	327	345	965
128		93-2	36-70	194	212	1227
129		93-3	36-71	188	206	1191
130		92-2	36-72	211	229	555
131		92-3	36-73	187	205	445
132		94-2	36-74	167	185	1944
133		93-4	36-75	249	267	969
134		94-1	36-76	215	233	500
135		94-4	37-77	380	398	133
136		94-3	37-78	291	309	804
137		96-1	37-79	350	368	958
138		96-2	37-80	234	252	389
139		96-4	37-81	298	316	219
140		97-1	37-82	330	348	1831
141		97-3	37-83	304	322	1594
142		98-1	37-84	136	154	187
143		100-1	38-85	263	281	1835
144		102-1	38-86	284	302	1717
145		101-4	38-87	288	306	1684
146		99-3	38-88	221	239	1500

Dîvân-i Kebîr Replica, Volume 2, Page 132a

Rubáiyát	Duplicate numbers	Ergin	Gölpinarli	Forûzânfar	Şefik Can	Farhadi Gamard
147		101-1	38-89	226	244	1420
148		101-2	38-90	313	331	1385
149		102-4	38-91	166	184	1202
150		103-3	38-92	383	401	268
151		103-2	38-93	323	341	1203
152		103-4	38-94	307	325	136
153		104-2	39-95	156	174	1170
154		103-1	39-96	425	443	1856
155		105-2	39-97	123	141	689
156		105-1	39-98	241	259	1527
157		106-2	39-99	151	169	1228
158		105-4	39-100	355	373	331

Rubáiyát	Duplicate numbers	Ergin	Gölpinarli	Forûzânfar	Şefik Can	Farhadi Gamard
159		106-1	39-101	354	372	613
160		106-4	40-102	164	182	1113
161		106-3	40-103	214	232	24
162		108-2	40-104	253	271	730
163		108-3	40-105	256	274	1243
164		109-3	40-106	393	411	1179
165		109-4	40-107	367	385	1225
166		110-1	40-108	301	319	852
167		110-3	40-109	400	418	186
168		111-1	41-110	237	255	1530
169		112-1	41-111	269	287	91
170		112-2	41-112	379	397	1430
171		112-3	41-113	257	275	987
172		112-4	41-114	325	343	1879
173		113-2	41-115	145	163	1591
174		113-4	41-116	359	377	144
175		114-3	41-117	289	307	1099
176		114-2	42-118	413	431	1219
177		115-3	42-119	124	142	469
178		115-4	42-120	418	436	1733
179		115-2	42-121	377	395	838

Dîvân-i Kebîr Replica, Volume 2, Page 132b

Rubáiyát	Duplicate numbers	Ergin	Gölpinarli	Forûzânfar	Şefik Can	Farhadi Gamard
180		115-1	42-122	147	165	1165
181		116-3	42-123	308	326	1807
182		116-1	42-124	410	428	913
183		117-2	42-125	396	414	1673
184		116-4	43-126	161	179	736
185		121-3	43-127	415	433	159
186		118-1	43-128	372	390	1281
187	1326	119-2	43-129	419	437	326
188		119-3	43-130	428	446	652
189		118-4	43-131	191	209	757
190		121-4	43-132	368	386	1295

Rubáiyát	Duplicate numbers	Ergin	Gölpinarli	Forûzânfar	Şefik Can	Farhadi Gamard
191		118-2	43-133	315	333	50
192		123-1	44-134	245	263	145
193		122-1	44-135	378	396	1766
194		104-3	44-136	247	265	264
195		123-3	44-137	401	419	1568
196		124-2	44-138	105	123	1456
197		124-3	44-139	225	243	1312
198		124-1	44-140	398	416	1491
199		125-4	44-141	417	435	683
200		126-2	45-142	111	129	395
201		126-4	45-143	177	195	516
202		128-1	45-144	207	225	900
203		127-1	45-145	246	264	636
204		127-3	45-146	422	440	1403
205		129-1	45-147	342	360	1728
206		129-4	45-148	264	282	1948
207		129-3	45-149	103	121	16
208		129-2	46-150	178	196	601
209		130-4	46-151	280	298	511
210		131-1	46-152	397	415	1685
211		130-3	46-153	165	183	1149
212		134-2	46-154	306	324	1362

Dîvân-i Kebîr Replica, Volume 2, Page 133a

Rubáiyát	Duplicate numbers	Ergin	Gölpinarli	Forûzânfar	Şefik Can	Farhadi Gamard
213	1352	131-3	46-155	365	383	664
214		132-2	46-156	272	290	132
215		133-1	46-157	258	276	398
216		133-3	47-158	251	269	923
217		132-1	47-159	336	354	1680
218		135-4	47-160	314	332	1264
219		136-3	47-161	364	382	36
220		136-1	47-162	238	256	244
221		137-3	67-1	430	485	455
222		138-1	67-2	432	487	1251

Rubáiyát	Duplicate numbers	Ergin	Gölpinarli	Forûzânfar	Şefik Can	Farhadi Gamard
223		137-4	67-3	431	486	721
224		155-3	67-1	666	720	1321
225		151-1	67-2	650	704	892
226		157-2	67-3	689	743	1903
227		155-2	68-4	652	706	285
228		157-1	68-5	653	707	1548
229		149-2	68-6	684	738	1616
230		148-1	68-7	658	712	22
231		149-4	68-8	735	788	1414
232		148-2	68-9	670	724	1415
233		148-4	68-10	673	727	1262
234		148-3	68-11	732	785	1508
235		149-1	68-12	678	732	1628
236		149-3	69-13	724	778	1909
237		149-1	69-14	661	715	31
238		144-1	69-15	660	714	1421
239	1811	141-2	69-16	659	713	1636
240		142-2	69-17	535	590	1780
241		138-4	69-18	718	772	1690
242		168-3	69-19	664	718	30
243		165-4	69-20	719	773	1463
244		166-3	69-21	729	782	1462
245	1766/1798	154-1	70-22	852	904	1047

Dîvân-i Kebîr Replica, Volume 2, Page 133b

246		166-2	70-23	728	781	1461
247		165-2	70-24	737	790	1915
248		166-1	70-25	842	894	1573
249		171-3	70-26	536	591	175
250		175-2	70-27	680	734	1534
251		175-3	70-28	654	708	1545
252		176-2	70-29	508	563	1344
253		179-3	70-30	739	792	1328
254		180-4	71-31	683	737	1625

Rubáiyát	Duplicate numbers	Ergin	Gölpinarli	Forûzânfar	Şefik Can	Farhadi Gamard
255		182-2	71-32	738	791	1898
256		185-1	71-33	693	747	1654
257		189-4	71-34	528	583	1096
258		198-2	71-35	685	739	1791
259		198-1	71-36	731	784	1907
260		198-3	71-37	726	780	1376
261		193-4	71-38	662	716	591
262		202-4	72-39	523	578	1033
263		205-4	72-40	734	787	427
264		206-3	72-41	538	593	1496
265		207-1	72-42	517	572	1723
266		210-1	72-43	745	798	1786
267		210-2	72-44	540	595	210
268		211-2	72-45	676	730	20
269		211-3	72-46	677	731	1751
270		214-3	72-47	730	783	1416
271		216-4	73-48	686	740	70
272		220-4	73-49	746	799	1418
273		219-2	73-50	688	742	1422
274	431	219-3	73-51	500	555	1575
275		222-3	73-52	675	729	1555
276		225-4	73-53	742	795	1836
277		225-3	73-54	687	741	1424
278		228-3	73-55	526	581	330

Dîvân-i Kebîr Replica, Volume 2, Page 134a

279		232-1	74-56	663	717	1438
280		231-3	74-57	533	588	149
281		231-4	74-58	534	589	148
282		233-2	74-59	674	728	1261
283		233-3	74-60	672	726	1148
284		233-1	74-61	736	789	1218
285		238-3	74-62	717	771	1404
286		199-1	74-63	668	722	1880

Rubáiyát	Duplicate numbers	Ergin	Gölpinarli	Forûzânfar	Şefik Can	Farhadi Gamard
287		241-1	75-64	667	721	1861
288		242-3	75-65	681	735	1349
289		245-3	75-66	725	779	978
290		244-4	75-67	741	794	1411
291	1773	248-4	75-68	783	835	1814
292		250-1	75-69	872	924	1074
293		163-2	75-70	838	890	1307
294		154-4	75-71	559	614	1579
295		153-3	75-72	505	560	771
296		154-3	76-73	557	612	1593
297		152-3	76-74	767	820	63
298		151-4	76-75	795	347	1426
299		152-1	76-76	551	606	1943
300	1500	167-2	76-77	785	837	1716
301		155-4	76-78	612	666	1877
302		153-1	76-79	816	868	1860
303		156-1	76-80	809	861	180
304		151-3	76-81	864	916	1973
305	1800	156-3	77-82	622	676	1812
306		158-1	77-83	763	816	93
307		158-2	77-84	757	810	464
308		157-3	77-85	648	702	84
309		159-1	77-86	629	683	770
310		158-4	77-87	497	552	710
311		158-3	77-88	493	548	1167

Dîvân-i Kebîr Replica, Volume 2, Page 134b

312		157-4	77-89	857	909	1141
313		139-2	77-90	649	703	418
314		160-4	78-91	477	532	10
315	1551	160-3	78-92	435	490	117
316		139-4	78-93	697	751	1024
317		140-2	78-94	531	586	865
318	1626	141-1	78-95	480	535	887

Rubáiyát	Duplicate numbers	Ergin	Gölpinarli	Forûzânfar	Şefik Can	Farhadi Gamard
319		141-4	78-96	848	900	1425
320		147-4	78-97	507	518	1332
321		145-1	78-98	812	864	1558
322		143-2	78-99	463	518	1926
323		150-1	79-100	827	879	616
324		143-1	79-101	546	601	921
325		140-4	79-102	611	665	1584
326		139-3	79-103	532	587	1205
327		143-3	79-104	584	639	933
328		143-4	79-105	555	609	1233
329		142-4	79-106	859	911	1540
330		147-1	79-107	696	750	110
331		145-2	79-108	452	507	638
332		146-2	80-109	506	561	1929
333		146-1	80-110	503	558	585
334		145-3	80-111	743	796	1710
335		162-3	80-112	858	910	1552
336		162-1	80-113	451	506	966
337		164-3	80-114	448	503	590
338		163-4	80-115	607	661	489
339		164-2	80-116	702	756	712
340		162-2	80-117	469	524	1057
341		169-2	81-118	468	523	64
342		139-1	81-119	462	517	672
343		161-2	81-120	437	492	104
344		167-4	81-121	550	605	1389

Dîvân-i Kebîr Replica, Volume 2, Page 135a

345		172-1	81-122	617	671	1402
346		170-2	81-123	627	681	1049
347		170-3	81-124	619	673	1574
348		170-4	81-125	708	762	1970
349		174-2	82-126	791	843	121
350		173-2	82-127	520	575	853

Rubáiyát	Duplicate numbers	Ergin	Gölpinarli	Forûzânfar	Şefik Can	Farhadi Gamard
351		173-4	82-128	810	862	1439
352		174-1	82-129	839	891	650
353		175-1	82-130	590	645	1792
354		175-4	82-131	579	634	1652
355		178-4	82-132	436	491	1077
356		177-2	82-133	496	551	1286
357		177-4	82-134	613	667	1030
358		176-1	83-135	630	684	1775
359		177-1	83-136	805	857	1467
360		172-2	83-137	764	817	1670
361		179-2	83-138	800	852	1837
362		179-4	83-139	616	670	2
363		180-3	83-140	804	856	1847
364		179-1	83-141	439	494	556
365		180-2	83-142	440	495	1501
366	1774	183-2	83-143	537	592	1199
367		184-2	84-144	595	649	1547
368		184-3	84-145	594	648	970
369		185-4	84-146	494	549	155
370		185-3	84-147	605	659	163
371		185-2	84-148	499	554	1632
372		186-1	84-149	715	769	410
373		186-3	84-150	458	513	1763
374		188-3	84-151	818	870	420
375		187-4	84-152	560	615	743
376		188-2	85-153	548	603	1878
377		186-4	85-154	443	498	834

Dîvân-i Kebîr Replica, Volume 2, Page 135b

378		188-4	85-155	710	764	1048
379		192-1	85-156	473	528	1423
380		190-3	85-157	592	646	1169
381		191-1	85-158	549	604	1514
382		190-4	85-159	569	624	1060

Rubáiyát	Duplicate numbers	Ergin	Gölpinarli	Forûzânfar	Şefik Can	Farhadi Gamard
383		191-2	85-160	706	760	143
384		195-4	86-161	581	---	1061
385		195-3	86-162	790	842	1554
386		200-1	86-163	714	768	347
387		200-2	86-164	834	886	1744
388		193-2	86-165	849	901	23
389		199-3	86-166	600	654	1885
390		193-3	86-187	774	826	1393
391		195-1	86-168	821	873	1917
392		197-2	86-169	593	647	1408
393		197-1	87-170	574	629	1928
394		195-2	87-171	830	882	1889
395		196-4	87-172	788	840	1590
396		201-4	87-173	636	690	610
397		201-3	87-174	502	557	1051
398		200-4	87-175	690	744	950
399		203-1	87-176	749	802	673
400		204-1	87-177	869	921	349
401		201-2	87-178	614	668	678
402		204-3	88-179	771	824	624
403		205-1	88-180	621	675	450
404		208-2	88-181	644	698	1669
405		207-3	88-182	703	757	754
406		206-4	88-183	633	687	8
407		206-2	88-184	492	547	574
408		208-1	88-185	543	598	1383
409		207-4	88-186	824	876	718
410		206-1	88-187	808	860	1790
Dîvân-i Kebîr Replica, Volume 2, Page 136a						
411		208-3	89-188	847	899	1541
412		209-3	89-189	691	745	486
413		208-4	89-190	756	809	1949
414		210-3	89-191	870	922	1715

Rubáiyát	Duplicate numbers	Ergin	Gölpinarli	Forûzânfar	Şefik Can	Farhadi Gamard
415		212-2	89-192	489	544	1283
416		212-1	89-193	577	632	1017
417		213-4	89-194	642	696	1748
418		213-1	89-195	461	516	1605
419		213-2	90-196	639	693	839
420		214-2	90-197	780	832	821
421		215-1	90-198	487	542	434
422		216-3	90-199	610	664	1872
423		216-1	90-200	434	489	690
424		216-2	90-201	704	758	55
425		215-3	90-202	521	576	1750
426		217-1	90-203	766	819	929
427		218-1	90-204	713	767	411
428		217-4	91-205	753	806	843
429		217-3	91-206	768	821	1311
430		220-3	91-207	598	---	1604
431	274	219-4	73-51	500	555	1575
432		220-2	91-208	699	753	1922
433		221-1	91-209	645	699	432
434		218-4	91-210	754	807	1474
435		218-3	91-211	556	611	1195
436		220-1	91-212	511	566	1597
437		221-4	91-213	467	522	1410
438		222-1	91-214	803	855	1081
439		223-1	92-215	588	643	935
440		224-1	92-216	811	863	1916
441		223-3	92-217	829	881	1827
442		226-3	92-218	589	644	1370
443		224-3	92-219	694	748	1639

Rubáiyát	Duplicate numbers	Ergin	Gölpinarli	Forûzânfar	Şefik Can	Farhadi Gamard
Dîvân-i Kebîr Replica, Volume 2, Page136b						
444		227-3	92-220	575	630	912
445		226-1	92-221	554	610	1361
446		228-1	92-222	618	672	1059
447		227-4	93-223	513	568	964
448		229-4	93-224	819	871	1972
449		231-2	93-225	580	635	1287
450		213-1	93-226	583	638	1544
451		230-4	93-227	567	622	1016
452		232-3	93-228	643	697	1749
453		232-2	93-229	759	812	146
454		234-2	93-230	485	540	283
455		233-4	93-231	441	496	1495
456		234-1	94-232	776	828	198
457	1631	235-3	94-233	585	640	1441
458		235-1	94-234	516	571	1153
459		234-4	94-235	464	519	1373
460		237-2	94-236	836	888	848
461		237-1	94-237	835	887	404
462		236-4	94-238	466	521	937
463		240-1	94-239	867	919	454
464		238-2	94-240	615	669	1224
465		239-3	95-241	655	709	628
466		237-4	95-242	545	600	1641

Bibliography: *Mevlânâ Rubâîler*

Can, Şefik. Hz. *Mevlânâ'nin Rubâîleri*. Ankara, Turkey: T.C. Kûltûr Bakanliği Yayinlari/2752 Yayimlar Dairesi Başkanliği Sanat-Ebediyat Esereleri Dizise/3655-120, 2001.

Forüzânfar, Badî'uzzamân, ed. *Kulliyât-é shams yâdiwân-é kabîr-e mawlânâ jalâluddîn Muhammad mashhûrba-mawlawî*. Tehrân: University of Tehrân, 1957-1967.

Gölpinarli, Abdülbakî. *Dîvân-i Kebîr Mevlânâ Celâleddîn*. I-VII. Ankara: Turkey: Kûltûr Bakanliği, 1992.

_____. *Mevlânâ Celâleddîn, Rubâîler*. Ankara: Turkey: Ajans-Tûrk Matbaacilik Sanayi, 1982.

Bibliography: *The Rubáiyát of Rumi, The Ergin Translations*

Ergin, Nevit Oguz & Eçkmekçioğlu, Merâl. *Mevlânâ Rubâîler*. Konya: Sarayonu Gazete-Matbaa, 2016.

―――――. *Private Notes*, 2015.

Erol, Erdoğan. *Mevlânâ's Life, Works and the Mevlânâ Museum*. Konya: Altunari Ofset Ltd. Şti, 2005.

Gamard, Ibrahim & Farhadi, Rawan. *The Quatrains of Rumi*. San Rafael, CA: Sufi Dari Books, 2008.

Rumi, Mevlânâ Celâleddîn. *Dîvân-i Kebîr, Meter 1*, Nevit O. Ergin, Translator. Walla Walla, WA: Turkish Ministry of Culture and Current, 1995.

―――――. *Dîvân-i Kebîr, Meter 8a*, Nevit O. Ergin, Translator. Los Angeles, CA: Turkish Ministry of Culture and Echo Publications, 1998.

―――――. *Dîvân-i Kebîr Replica*. Compiled by Hasan ibni Osman-al Mavlavi, (1367-68). Konya: Altunari Ofset Ltd. Şti., 2007.

Shushud, Hasan. *Fakir Sözleri*. Bloomfield Hills, MI: Private Collection of Nevit Ergin, 1982.

Nevit O. Ergin
(1928-2015)

Nevit Ergin's country of birth was Turkey. Although he continued to take frequent trips to his home country, he lived the majority of his adult life in the United States, first in Michigan and then in Southern and finally Northern California. He was a plastic surgeon. He is survived by five children and three grandchildren.

Dr. Ergin devoted himself to the same spiritual path as Rumi. The last 25 years of his life were used to bring more of Rumi's poetry and more awareness of Rumi's message to the Western world. Ergin's English translations are from the Turkish translations of Turkish scholar Abdülbakî Gölpinarli, and they are inspired. He was able to capture the essence of every verse he translated... and he translated over 44,000 verses.

As he liked to say, Ergin spent 60 years of his life "trying to get rid of this Earth before it gets rid of me."

Other Works by Nevit O. Ergin

Crazy As We Are

The Dîvân-i Kebîr of Mevlânâ Celâleddîn Rumi
(Translation in 22 Volumes)

Divine Wine

Forbidden Rumi (with Will Johnson)

The Glory of Absence

Insane with Love (with Will Johnson)

Magnificent One

A Rose Garden

Mevlânâ Rubâîler (with Merâl Eçkmekçioğlu)

The Sufi Path of Annihilation

Tales of a Modern Sufi

Unknown Rumi

For those who would be interested in knowing Ergin's views on Rumi's quatrains, *Unknown Rumi* is a selection of 100 of the quatrains, with comments by Ergin on each of them.

Millicent Alexander
(1947-)

Millicent Alexander was born and raised in Los Angeles, California. She met Nevit Ergin at the home of Hasan Shushud in Istanbul, Turkey, in 1972. An account of her first meeting with these two remarkable men is included in *The Sufi Path of Annihilation* by Nevit O. Ergin (Inner Traditions).

That meeting was also her introduction to Itlak Yolu, the Sufi Path of Annihilation and Absolute Liberation, which embraces the universality of Rumi's messages. She has stayed on that path ever since.

She also stayed life-long friends with Nevit Ergin, working with him on bringing Rumi's poetry to the English-speaking world from 1992 (with the publication of *Crazy As We Are* [Holm Press]) until his passing in 2015.

Ms. Alexander is a retired educator and currently lives in Los Angeles, California.

Shahzad Mazhar
(1970-)

Shahzad Mazhar was born in Lahore, Pakistan. For his schooling, he was sent to St. Mary's Academy and finished his high school at Forman Christian College, Lahore. He was first exposed to Urdu and Persian poetry by his father, who was an officer in the Pakistani army. After high school, he traveled to the U.S.A. to study engineering. He was a partner in a computer manufacturing company in his twenties and thirties.

His interest in Rumi since his early twenties exposed him to the translations of Dr. Nevit Ergin. Further inquiry brought him into contact with Millicent Alexander, who provided him with the opportunity to be part of a team bringing Ergin's translations to the world, translations of the extraordinary poetry of the spiritual Master known in the West as Rumi.

A Final Note

Fall into the bottomless abyss, so that like the heavenly bodies, you may be free from falling.
                                    -Hasan Lutfi Shushud
                                    Fakir Sözleri, 16.

www.ingramcontent.com/pod-product-compliance
Lightning Source LLC
Chambersburg PA
CBHW070049080526
44586CB00013B/973